The Practice Papers

GCSE Biology

Ron Pickering

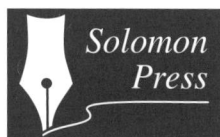

Solomon Press

Published by Solomon Press
Unit 1, Rydon Farm, West Newton
Somerset, TA7 0BZ
Tel: 01278 661 300
Email: info@solomon-press.com

Web site: www.solomon-press.com

The Homework Series is a trade mark of Solomon Press

© R Pickering 2001
First published 2001

ISBN 1 901724 20 4

Design and typesetting by Pedeke Ltd, Bridgwater, Somerset
Printed in Great Britain by The Friary Press, Dorchester, Dorset

Contents

1 - LIVING THINGS AND THEIR ACTIVITIES

CELLS, TISSUES AND ORGANS

1   Animals and plants are made up of cells, tissues and organs.
This list contains some cells, tissues and organs:

Phagocyte, sperm, epidermis, xylem, liver, blood, heart, leaf, ileum, ovary, neurone, brain, stem

Make a table with these headings :

Cell	Tissue	Organ

Place each of the structures from the list into the correct column.   *(13)*

2   These diagrams show a human muscle cell and a palisade cell from a leaf.
Many of the structures in these cells are labelled with code letters.

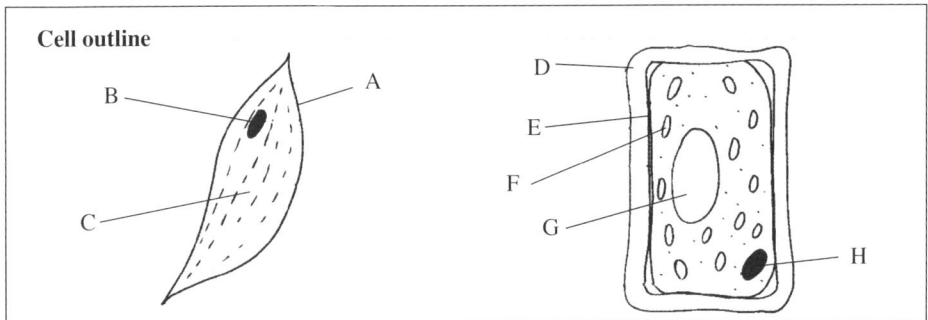

Use the code letters to identify

a   two structures found in both cells   *(2)*
b   a structure found in a muscle cell which allows it to control the activities of the cell *(1)*
c   a structure in the palisade cell which allows it to carry out photosynthesis   *(1)*
d   a structure in the palisade cell which is made of cellulose   *(1)*
e   a structure in the muscle cell which is not found in a red blood cell   *(1)*
f   What is meant by the term 'cell specialisation'?   *(2)*

3   Arrange these biological terms in order of size (from the smallest to the largest)

Organ, cell, organism, organelle, tissue, system   *(3)*

4   **a**   Arrange these units of length in order, from largest to smallest.

Kilometre, micrometre, metre, millimetre   *(2)*

b   An average plant cell is 50 micrometres long.
How many plant cells could fit into one millimetre? Show your working.   *(1)*

5   Copy this table.
    Complete the table by placing a tick if the structure is present and a cross if it is not.

Structure	Liver cell	Palisade cell
Cell surface membrane		
Chloroplasts		
Cytoplasm		
Cellulose cell wall		
Nucleus		
Starch granule		
Glycogen granule		
Large, permanent vacuole		

(16)

6   Use words from this list to complete the following paragraphs.
    The words may be used once, more than once, or not at all.

palisade cell, epidermis, tissues, excretory system, specialised, cells, blood, kidney, chloroplasts, leaf, red blood cell, division of labour, xylem, phloem, nervous, systems, endocrine, organ

a   Large numbers of .... that have the same structure and function
    are grouped together to form ...., for example
    .... Several separate tissues may be joined together to form an
    .... which is a complex structure capable of performing a particular
    task with great efficiency. In the most highly developed organisms these complex
    structures may work together in .... , for example the
    .... in humans is responsible for the removal of the waste
    products of metabolism.

(6)

b   The structure of cells may be highly adapted to perform one function, i.e. the cells may
    become .... One excellent example is the
    .... which is highly adapted to carry oxygen in
    mammalian blood. If the different cells, tissues and organs of a multicellular organism
    perform different functions they are said to show ....
    One consequence of this is the need for close co-ordination between different organs –
    this function is performed by the .... and
    .... systems in mammals.

(5)

c   In plants an example of a cell highly specialised for photosynthesis is the
    .... which contains many .... These
    cells are located in the organ called the .... which also contains other
    tissues such as .... which limits water loss and
    .... which transports water and mineral ions to the leaf.

(5)

1 Use words from this list to complete the following sentences.
You may use each word once, more than once or not at all.

fatty acids, glycogen, glucose, sucrose, glycerol, amino acids, haemoglobin, simple sugars.

a Starch consists of smaller units called .... The sugar most often
used for sweetening foods is called ....

b Fats are made up of smaller units called .... and ....

c Proteins are made of smaller units called .... – an important
protein in the human body is ....   *(6)*

2 Copy and complete this table. Place '+' if the element is present and '–' if it is absent
from the molecules listed: *(3)*

	Carbon	Hydrogen	Oxygen	Calcium	Nitrogen
Carbohydrate					
Fat					
Protein					

3 Food contains biological molecules. It can be important to know exactly which molecules
are present in which foods.
There are chemical tests called *Food tests* that allow us to find this out.

The boxes below list certain molecules and food tests.

A	Protein	Biuret
B	Simple sugar	Iodine solution
C	Fat	Biuret
D	Starch	Benedict's reagent
E	Protein	Alcohol emulsion
F	Starch	Iodine solution
G	Fat	Alcohol emulsion
H	Simple sugar	Benedict's reagent

a The molecules and the chemical tests are only correctly matched in four of the boxes.
Write down the letters of these four boxes.   *(4)*

b Describe exactly how you would carry out a Benedict's test if you were given a
powdered sample of a food.
Be sure to include any safety measures you would take.   *(3)*

6

4   Five test tubes were set up and reagents added as shown

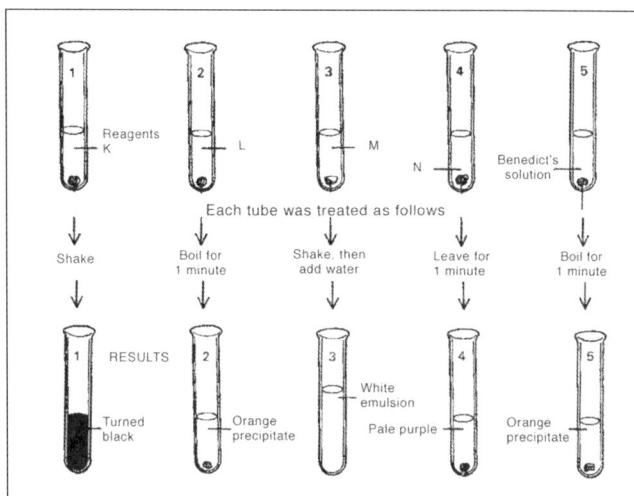

a   Name the reagents K, L, M and N.   *(4)*
b   State the type of biological molecule found in each of the tubes 1 to 5.   *(5)*
c   A student wants to test five different cereals for the presence of sugar.
    Explain why it is important that he uses the same volume of reagent and boils the
    mixture for the same length of time on each occasion.   *(2)*

5   This bar chart shows the percentage of each of the main elements in the human body.

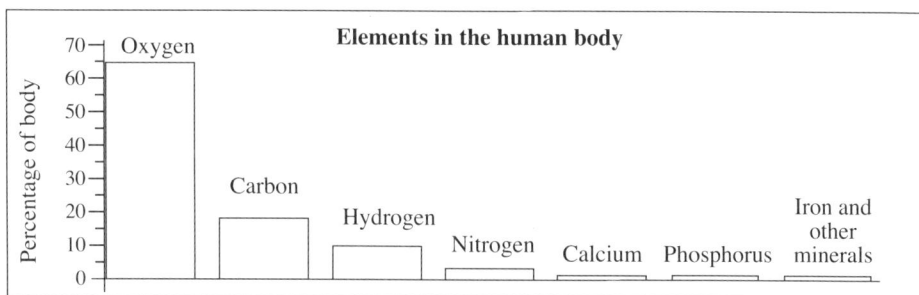

a   Convert this information: **i** into a table, and **ii** into a pie chart   *(5)*
b   Which do you think is the best way to show this data? Explain why.   *(2)*
c   These elements are largely present as molecules.
    The proportions of the main molecules in a human body are approximately:

      Fats 14%, Proteins 12%, Carbohydrates 1.0%, Water 70%

    i   Which is the most abundant molecule?   *(1)*
    ii   Which molecule contains most of the nitrogen?   *(1)*
    iii   Which molecule contains most of the oxygen?   *(1)*
    iv   Which molecule contains most of the carbon?   *(1)*
    v   The percentages for these molecules do not total 100%.
              Suggest another organic compound which is part of the remainder.   *(1)*
    vi   Which structure(s) in the body contain most of the calcium?   *(1)*

1   The cells of the epidermis of the rhubarb stem contain a red pigment.
    This pigment makes it easy to see the cytoplasm in these cells, and to observe how
    the cytoplasm and cell membrane are affected by the external environment.

    Strips of rhubarb epidermis were placed in three different sucrose solutions.
    The strips were left in the solutions for 30 minutes, and the cells observed under
    the high power objective lens of a light microscope.
    The observations are recorded in the table below:

Solution	Appearance
A	Cell membrane pulled away from cell wall. No visible vacuole.
B	Cell membrane pushed firmly against cell wall. Large vacuole near centre of cell.
C	No change from 'normal' appearance - cell membrane just touching cell wall. Medium-sized vacuole in centre of cell

    a   Name the process responsible for these changes in the cells' appearance.   *(1)*
    b   What term is used to describe the cell membrane that allows this process
        to occur?   *(1)*
    c   What has happened to cause the cell membrane and cytoplasm to push against
        the cell wall in solution B?   *(1)*
    d   What can you say about solution C to explain the appearance of the cells?   *(1)*
    e   Copy the diagram below. Complete it, and add labels to show the cell
        membrane, cytoplasm and vacuole of a cell placed in solution A.   *(3)*

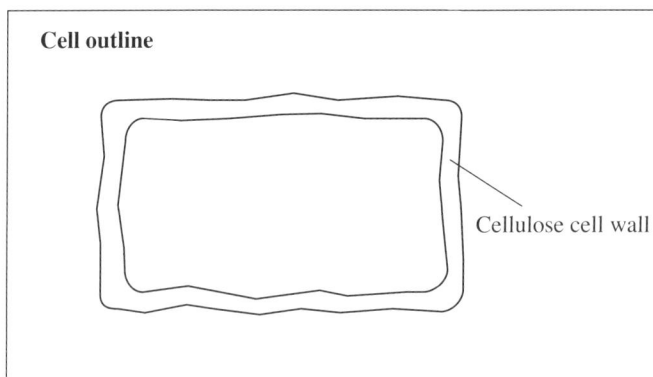

Cell outline

Cellulose cell wall

2   Use words from this list to complete the paragraphs on the next page.
    You may use each word once, more than once or not at all.   *(14)*

    diffusion, osmosis, photosynthesis, active transport, cell wall, swell, shrink, partially-
    permeable membrane, cytoplasm, respiration, oxygen, glycogen, carbon dioxide, amino
    acids, pathway, energy, along, against, concentration gradient, epidermis

Animal cells contain ...., a semi-fluid solution of salts and other molecules, and are surrounded by a .... When surrounded by distilled water, the animal cells .... because the cell has a .... water potential than the surrounding water. Plant cells do not have this problem because they are surrounded by a ....

In the gut soluble food substances such as .... cross the gut lining into the capillaries by the process of .... , which is the movement of molecules down a .... When an equilibrium is reached between the gut contents and the blood, glucose may continue to be moved using the process called .... , which consumes .... and can move molecules .... a concentration gradient.

The leaves of green plants obtain the gas ...., which they require for the process of photosynthesis, by the process of .... They also lose the gas oxygen, produced during .... by the same process.

3 In an investigation to measure the speed of diffusion, cubes of gelatin which had been stained purple with an indicator solution were placed in dilute acid as shown in the diagram.

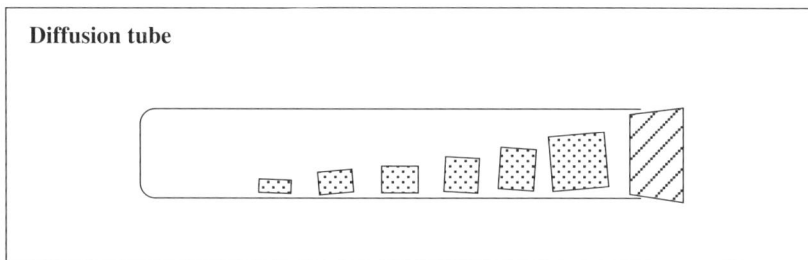

Diffusion tube

The time taken for each cube to change to an orange colour is shown in the table.

Length of side of cube/mm	Time taken to turn orange/s	Surface area of cube / mm² (total of 6 sides)	Volume of cube/ mm³	Surface area to volume ratio
1	20			
2	41			
3	76			
4	104			
5	188			
10	600			

a Copy and complete the table, and plot a graph of the surface area to volume ratio against the time taken to turn orange. (10)

b What do the results suggest about the efficiency of diffusion in supplying materials to the centre of an organism's body? (3)

c Suggest methods that animals use to improve the supply of oxygen to their cells by diffusion. (3)

9

1 Use words from this list to complete the following paragraph about enzymes.
You may use each word once, more than once or not at all.

pathways, enzymes, catalysts, activators, proteins, unusual, specific, denatured, destroyed

Enzymes are .... which speed up the biochemical .... in
living organisms. The enzymes themselves are not changed in these reactions, that is
they are biological ....
Enzymes are .... - each of them controls only one type of reaction. They
are .... by high temperatures and by extremes of pH.   *(5)*

2 In an experiment, apparatus is used to measure the effect of one factor, the **manipulated**
or **independent** variable, on the value of a second factor, the **responding** or **dependent**
variable. To be sure that the experiment is a fair test, all other factors must be kept
constant – these are **fixed** variables.

For example, a simple closed manometer
may be used to measure the effect of
temperature on the activity of the enzyme
catalase.

Closed manometer

Manometer to collect oxygen

Thermometer

Scale

Glass vessel in water bath

Disc of potato

Buffer solution and hydrogen peroxide

a what is the manipulated (independent)
variable in this experiment?
b Suggest two fixed variables, and
explain how the experimenter could
keep them constant.
c What is the responding variable in this
experiment?
How could it be measured?
d Suggest a suitable control for this
experiment.
e Students using this apparatus collected
five sets of data, and used them to calculate a mean.
How does this improve the validity of the results?   *(7 x 1)*

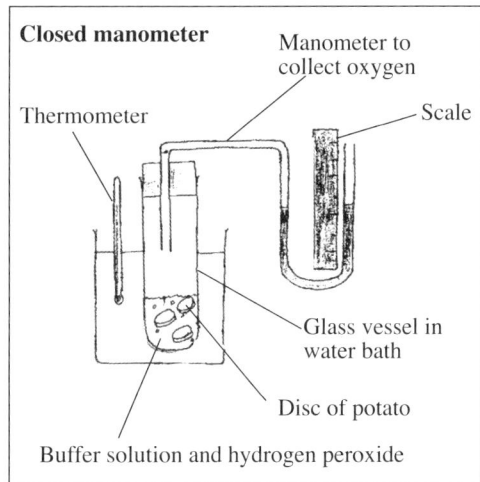

3 Using the apparatus shown above a student investigated the effect of temperature on the
activity of the enzyme catalase. He obtained these results:

Temperature/ºC	Time taken to evolve 10cm³ of oxygen/sec	Rate of oxygen release/ cm³ per sec
15	50	
25	25	
35	5	
45	20	
55	60	
65	150	
75	No gas evolved	

a Complete the table by calculating the rate of catalase activity. *(7)*
b Present the data in the form of a graph. *(5)*
c Explain the shape of the graph. *(4)*

4   In an experiment to measure the effect of pH on enzyme activity, pepsin (a protease) was mixed with solutions of different pH values. The mixture was then placed in a hole cut in the centre of a dish of gelatin. Gelatin is a protein, and can be stained with a coloured dye. When the pepsin digests the protein jelly a clear zone forms. The appearance of the plates at the start of the experiment, and after a period of 24 hours is shown.

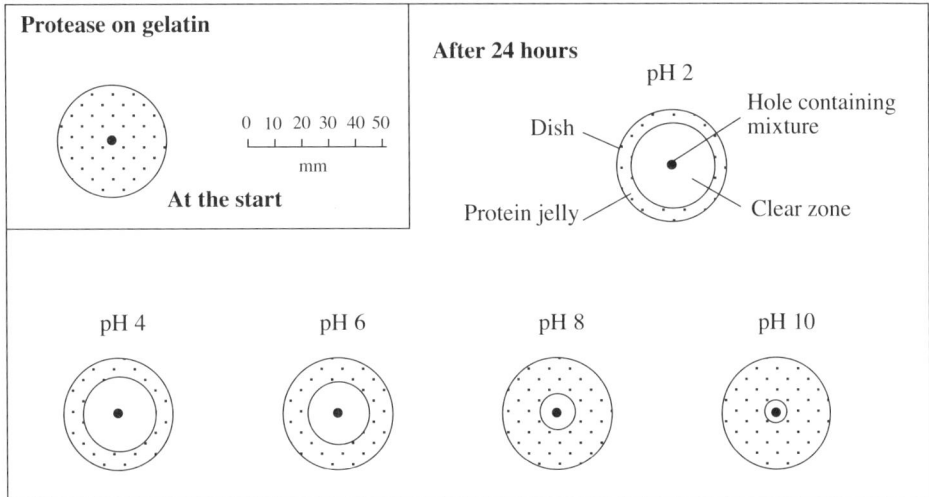

a Measure the diameters of the clear zones, and record them in a suitable table. *(5)*
b What is the best pH for the activity of pepsin? *(1)*
c This experiment was carried out at room temperature - about 20°C.
    What do you think might happen if the experiment is carried out at 30°C? *(2)*
d Apart from temperature, state one other factor which must be kept constant throughout the experiment. *(1)*

5   Respiration is the process that releases energy in cells. It also depends on enzymes. A group of students were interested in the effects of temperature on the rate of oxygen consumption by maggots. They obtained these results:

Temperature/°C	Oxygen consumption/mm per s
15	0.3
25	0.6
35	1.1
45	0.8
55	0.2
65	0.0

a plot these results in the form of a graph, and explain the shape of the curve. *(6)*
b In this investigation, identify the manipulated variable and the responding variable. Suggest any fixed variables. *(4)*

1 Complete the following paragraph. Use terms from the list below - you may use each term once, more than once or not at all.

anaerobic, moist, living cells, animals, glucose, aerobic, oxygen, carbon dioxide, heat, water, energy.

Respiration is a process which occurs in all .... The raw materials are .... and, sometimes, ... The purpose of the process is to release ...., and it is more efficient under .... conditions.   *(5)*

2 Respiration is a feature of living organisms.
Make a list of five other characteristics of living organisms.   *(5)*

3 The diagram shows how much energy is required for various activities.
The figures are given in kilojoules (kJ) per hour.

Energy for activity

Sleeping 300

Standing 450

Walking 1000

Schoolwork 650

Running 2200

Swimming 3200

   a Plot this information on a bar chart.   *(4)*
   b During a typical school day Sam stood for 1 hour, walked for 1 hour, ran for 1 hour and did school work for 4 hours. How much energy did he use?   *(2)*
   c Sleeping uses 300 kJ in one hour.
      Why is energy needed during periods of sleeping?   *(2)*
   d Suggest why swimming uses more energy than running   *(2)*

4 Heat is a form of energy, and is always released when the body is working.
When energy is released from the chemical energy stored in food, some of it is released as heat which is given off from the bodies of the respiring organisms.

The apparatus in the diagram is set up.

In one flask is a measured mass of germinating peas (these have been soaked for a day so that they start to germinate). In the second flask is an equal mass of peas which have been boiled to kill them. Both sets of peas are washed in disinfectant before they are sealed into the flasks.

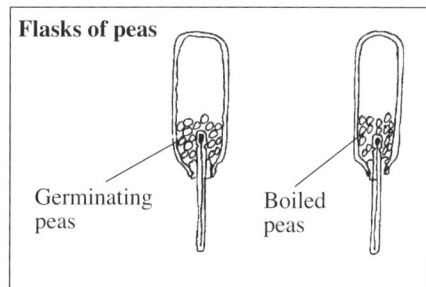

Flasks of peas

Germinating peas

Boiled peas

The temperature of the flask contents is noted at the start of the investigation, and again 48 hours later.

a Which flask showed the higher temperature at the end of the experiment?
Explain your answer. *(2)*

b Why is it important to sterilise the surface of the peas with disinfectant? *(1)*

c Why are the flasks not completely filled with peas? *(1)*

d Why is an equal mass of peas placed in each of the flasks?
Do you think that the mass of peas is the same at the end of the investigation?
Explain your answer. *(3)*

e Not all of the energy released during the peas' respiration is released as heat.
Suggest what happens to the rest of it. *(1)*

5 There are a number of ways of measuring carbon dioxide release by respiring organisms.
Each relies on noting a visible effect of carbon dioxide on an *indicator solution*.
One solution that is affected by carbon dioxide is *hydrogencarbonate indicator*, which is purple at high pH, red around neutral pH and orange-yellow at low pH.

This apparatus was set up to investigate the respiration of small animals.

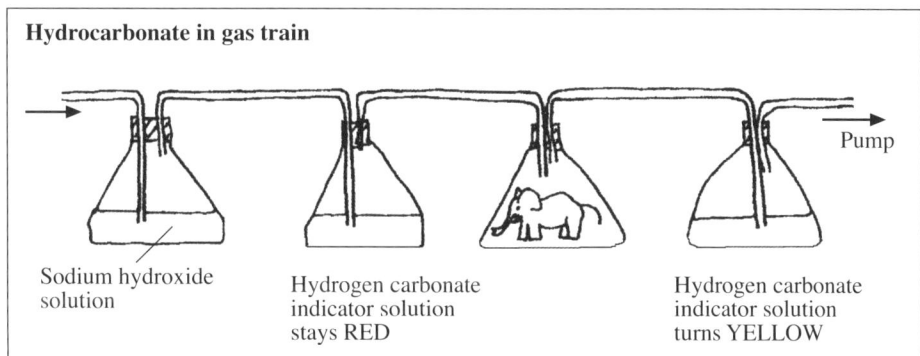

Hydrocarbonate in gas train

Sodium hydroxide solution

Hydrogen carbonate indicator solution stays RED

Hydrogen carbonate indicator solution turns YELLOW

Pump

a What is the purpose of the sodium hydroxide solution?
(N.B. potassium hydroxide would do just as well) *(1)*

b What does the indicator solution in flask B show? *(1)*

c How can you explain the change in flask D? *(1)*

d Suggest a control for this investigation, and explain why it is a suitable control. *(2)*

e Suggest any visible change to the flask C. Explain your answer. *(2)*

6 Here are a number of statements about aerobic respiration.
State whether each of them is True or False.

Aerobic respiration:

a uses water

b always requires oxygen

c occurs only in animal cells

d releases energy

e produces carbon dioxide

f is controlled by enzymes

g must have sugar as a starting material

h releases heat

i releases water

j is affected by temperature

k occurs in all living cells *(11 × 1)*

ECOLOGY AND ECOSYSTEMS

1   Use words from the following list to complete the paragraphs about ecosystems.
You may use each word once, more than once or not at all.   *(10)*

*respiration, decomposition, producer, chemical, carnivore, consumer, photosynthesis,
energy, light, elements, decomposers, herbivore.*

In each ecosystem there are many feeding relationships. A food chain represents a flow of
.... through an ecosystem, and always begins with an organism called a
.... which is able to trap .... energy and convert it to
.... energy. An organism of this type is eaten by a ...., which is
a kind of .... that feeds only on plant material. This type of organism is, in turn,
eaten by a .... (an organisms that consumes other animals).

The process in which light energy is transferred into a chemical form is called
.... – eventually the energy is released from its chemical form during the
process of .... This process provides energy for all living organisms, including
.... which are microbes that feed on the remains of animals and plants.

2   This diagram represents the number of different organisms in a certain food chain:

a   What name is given to this type of
    diagram?   *(1)*
b   Study the diagram and suggest
    organisms that could be at levels 2
    and 3.   *(2)*
c   Why are there fewer organisms at
    level 3 than level 2?   *(2)*

Pyramid of numbers

Level 4	Tawny Owl
Level 3	
Level 2	
Level 1	Grass seeds

d   Draw a similar diagram for the food
    chain

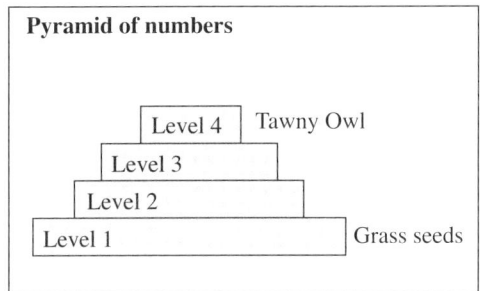

Oak tree ⇒ aphid ⇒ blue tit ⇒ sparrowhawk

Explain why this diagram is not identical to the one shown above.   *(4)*

3   The Antarctic Ocean provides a habitat for
a variety of organisms. This food web
shows the feeding relationships between
some of these organisms.

a   Which one of the organisms is a
    producer?   *(1)*
b   What is the name of the process that
    provides energy for this food web? *(1)*

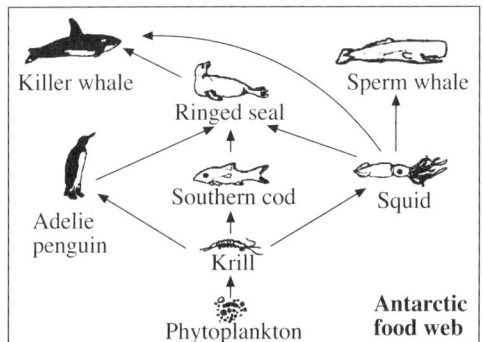

Antarctic food web: Killer whale, Ringed seal, Sperm whale, Adelie penguin, Southern cod, Squid, Krill, Phytoplankton

c Which organism would you expect to find in the largest numbers?
Explain your answer. *(3)*

d From this food web draw out a food chain that involves **five** organisms. *(2)*

e Large quantities of krill are caught and used as a food for farm animals.
  i Suggest an advantage to humans of this practice. *(1)*
  ii Suggest a disadvantage to the environment of this practice. *(1)*

4 Some students carried out a survey of the animals feeding on an oak tree. They collected a number of different species, and observed which animals fed on leaves and which fed on other animals. The results of their survey are shown in the table below:

Animal collected/observed	Number recorded	Food eaten by animal
Willow warbler	5	Larvae of winter moths and oak eggars
Winter moth larva	44	Oak leaves
Oak eggar caterpillar	53	Oak leaves
Tawny owl	2	Willow warblers, great tits and field mice
Great tit	5	Larvae of winter moths and oak eggars
Beetle	4	Larvae of winter moths and oak eggars
Field mouse	3	Acorns

a Copy the following table. Use the information above to name the animals in the trophic (feeding) levels in this table. *(2)*

Trophic level	Organisms present
4 : tertiary consumers	
3 : secondary consumers	
2 : primary consumers	
producer	

b Calculate how many animals there were at each trophic level.
Draw a table of your results. *(2)*

c Use a piece of graph paper to draw an accurate pyramid of numbers for the animals at the three trophic levels. *(4)*

d Why is the number of tertiary consumers not really representative of this particular oak tree ecosystem? *(2)*

5 A student wished to investigate the population of springtails, a small arthropod, in the soil beneath different types of tree. The teacher suggested using quadrats and a Tullgren funnel, and the investigation was carried out as shown in the diagram below.

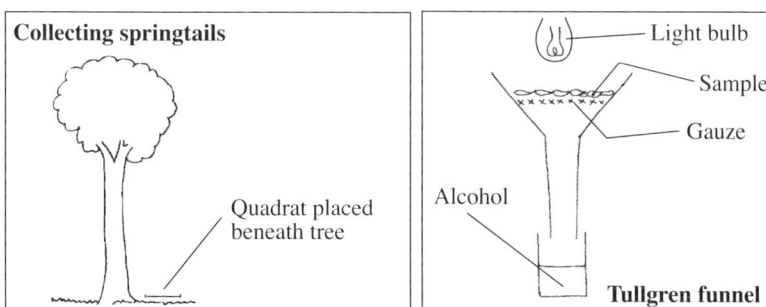

The student took an equal volume of soil from the centre of each quadrat, and then used the Tullgren Funnel to estimate the number of springtails in each sample.

a The quadrats were distributed in a random way. Why was this important? *(1)*
b The student used the same-sized sample from each quadrat – why? *(2)*
c The Tullgren funnel has a lamp and wire mesh as important parts.
   What functions do they have? *(2)*

The results of the investigation are shown in the table below

Number of springtails in sample	
Oak tree in woodland – fallen leaves beneath	Oak tree in parkland – fallen leaves removed
30	10
20	15
45	15
10	5
25	5
25	8
25	12
40	12
15	7
25	11

d Calculate the mean springtail numbers in the two different habitats. *(2)*

Oak leaves decompose and release a weak acid. The decomposition process generates heat and water. Decomposing leaves are a food source for many arthropods.

e Suggest one factor which might be responsible for the different number of springtails in the two habitats. Describe how you would measure this factor.
   How could you improve the investigation to eliminate the other factors which might affect the springtail numbers? *(6)*

6 Read the following passage.

In any ecosystem there is a *flow* of energy along food chains but a *cycling* of elements such as carbon and nitrogen. Carbon is an important element since it is found in all organic molecules – it is circulated between living organisms and their environment through the processes of respiration and photosynthesis.

The atmosphere contains about 0.03% carbon dioxide but this is increasing. It is believed that the cutting down of forests reduces the amount of carbon dioxide removed by photosynthesis, and the burning of wood and fossil fuels increases the atmospheric concentration of this gas. Most fossil fuels – such as oil, coal, peat and gas – were made from the bodies of dead organisms during the Carboniferous period about 350 million years ago. The bodies of these organisms did not decay because of the conditions surrounding them after death – very damp, anaerobic conditions do not allow decay to occur, for example. Later, the remains of these organisms were heated and subjected to pressure by Earth movements and the fossil fuels were formed.

When fossil fuels are burned both energy and carbon dioxide are released. It is thought that both heat energy and the carbon dioxide contribute to Global Warming. Global Warming may be responsible for changing weather patterns, such as severe rainstorms and high winds. These may dramatically affect ecosystems, by flooding for example.

This diagram shows the carbon cycle:

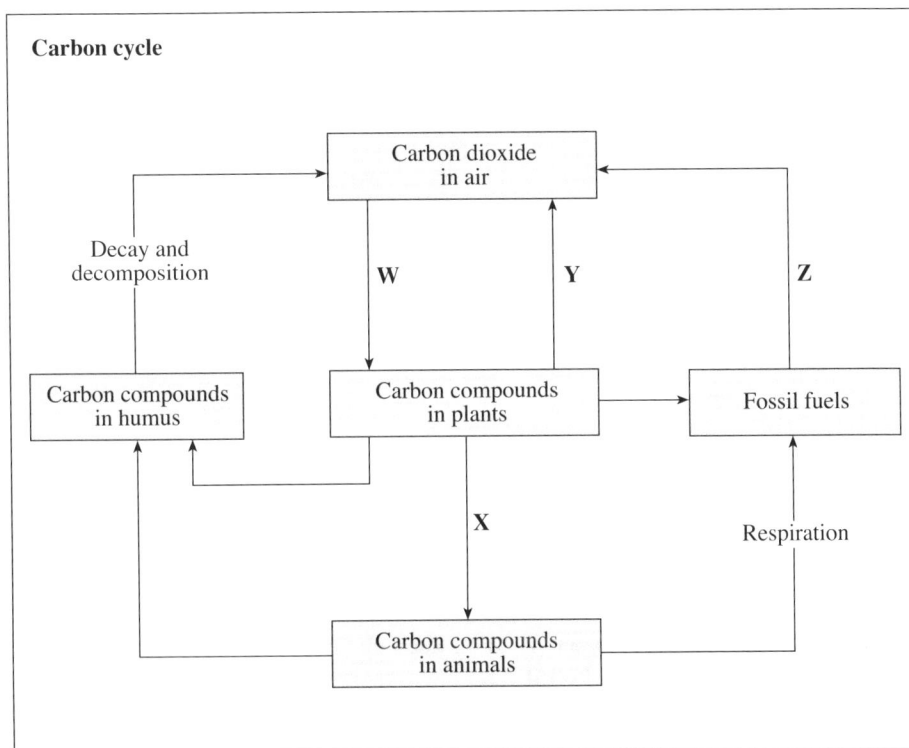

a Write an equation for photosynthesis. *(2)*
b Name the pigment required for trapping of light energy in photosynthesis. *(1)*
c What effect does cutting down forests have on atmospheric carbon dioxide levels? *(1)*
d Forest waste is often burned to clear land for farming.
   How does this burning affect the carbon dioxide content of the atmosphere? *(1)*
e Name the two main groups of organisms responsible for decay and decomposition. *(2)*
f State two benefits to plants of decomposition in an ecosystem. *(2)*
g Identify the processes labelled W, X, Y and Z in the diagram. *(4)*
h Suggest one effect on the environment of the burning of fossil fuels, apart
   from affecting the composition of the atmosphere. *(1)*

1 This diagram shows part of the nitrogen cycle.

Nitrogen cycle

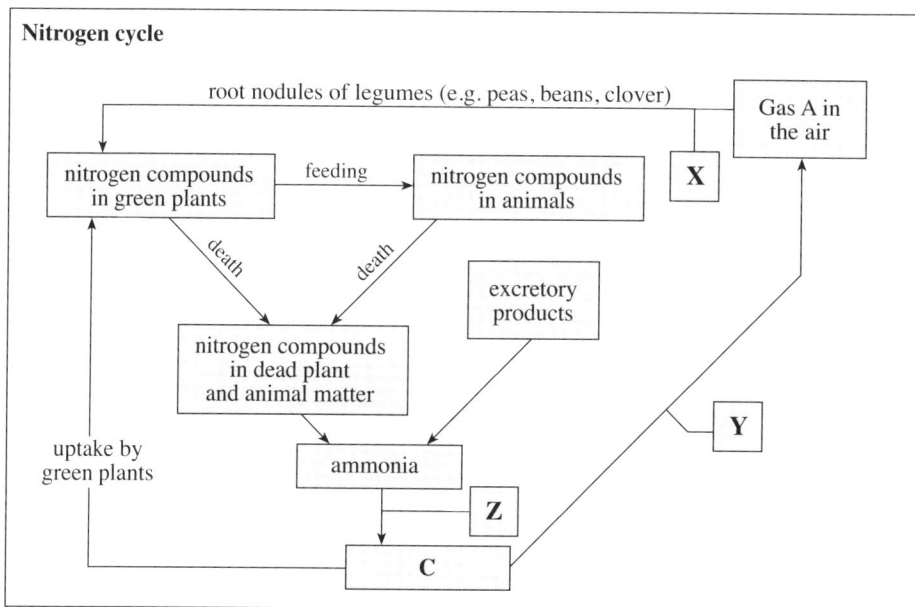

a Identify the gas labelled A. *(1)*
b Many of the stages of the nitrogen cycle depend on the actions of bacteria.
   Three of these processes are nitrification, nitrogen fixation and denitrification.
   Match up the labels X, Y and Z with these three processes. *(3)*
c Identify the compound labelled C *(1)*
d Name one biological molecule which is made by plants from compound C *(1)*
e Animal excretory products are broken down in the nitrogen cycle.
   Name one animal excretory product containing nitrogen. *(1)*

2 In order to increase the yield of crops, many farmers have used some or all of the following practices.

   A cutting down hedges
   B increasing the use of nitrate fertilisers
   C burning stubble after harvesting
   D draining of wet fields
   E repeatedly growing the same crop in the same field
   F deep ploughing of soil using heavy machinery

Many conservationists believe that these techniques may be damaging to the environment. Choose any two of the above and state how they help the farmer to increase the yield of crop, then choose three other techniques and explain how they might damage the environment.

Write your answers in a table like the one on the next page *(5)*

Technique	Benefit to farmer

Technique	Harm to the environment

3 *Bacteria and the nitrogen cycle*

Two students were investigating the ability of soil bacteria to convert ammonium ions to nitrate. They set up nine containers with equal volumes of soil, and added a fixed volume of ammonium sulphate solution to the soil. The containers were then incubated at a series of temperatures for 24 hours. After this period of time the soil in each of the containers was 'washed' with distilled water and the 'washings' were tested for the presence of nitrate. The results are shown in the Table below

Temperature/ $^\circ$C	Nitrate concentration/ arbitrary units
0	11
10	35
20	65
30	93
40	92
50	61
60	30
70	4
80	2

a Plot these results in the form of a graph. *(5)*

b Use your knowledge of the nitrogen cycle to explain the shape of the graph. *(3)*

c Why did the students incubate equal volumes of soil with equal volumes of ammonium sulphate solution for equal lengths of time? *(2)*

d The class teacher suggested some improvements to the experiment:

i Include a container to which no ammonium sulphate solution (just an equal volume of water) in the experiment

ii Include a container containing an equal volume of soil which had been pre-heated to 150°C in the experiment

What additional information could the results with these containers provide? *(4)*

e The father of one of the students was a farmer.

He asked to student to investigate whether waterlogging was affecting the nitrate levels in one of his fields.

How could you modify (change) this experiment to allow the student to provide this information? *(5)*

1   The table shows the number of rats caught in a suburban area between 1975 and 1980.

Year	Number caught	
	Males	females
1975	235	167
1976	279	198
1977	190	120
1978	115	94
1979	122	93
1980	160	110

a   Draw a bar chart of the male and female rats caught in this area
     between 1975 and 1980.   (4)
b   In which year were most rats caught?   (1)
c   Warfarin, a rat poison that works by preventing blood clotting, was first
     used on this population in the winter of 1976.
     What effect did it have on the rat population?   (2)
d   Suggest a reason for the changes in rat population from 1979 onwards. (2)
e   Rats are attracted to open rubbish tips, where they scavenge for food.
     How can rat numbers be controlled without trapping or poisoning them? (2)
f   Why are rats considered to be a health hazard?   (2)

2   Complete the following paragraphs about pollution of the atmosphere.
     Use terms from the following list - you may use each term once, more than
     once, or not at all.   (12)

*pests, CFC's, ultraviolet light, mesophyll, carbon dioxide, infra-red, methane, nitrogen,
cancer, photosynthesis, mutation, ozone*

The greenhouse effect may cause global warming when .... radiation is trapped
close to the Earth's surface by a layer of ....from ruminants, ...from
aerosols and ....from the combustion of fossil fuels. Global warming may allow
................to extend their range, but may have the benefit of increasing production of food
by ....

Holes in the ozone layer may result from ...., formerly used as refrigerants.
These holes allow the entry of too much ....radiation, which may lead to
skin................and an increased rate of ....(especially dangerous as these
may be passed on to the offspring of the affected person). The production of excess
...................may also be damaging - for example, photosynthesis is reduced when the
leaf ....is damaged.

3 This diagram shows the sequence of events associated with acid rain pollution. Complete the diagram using terms chosen from the list A to G. *(5)*

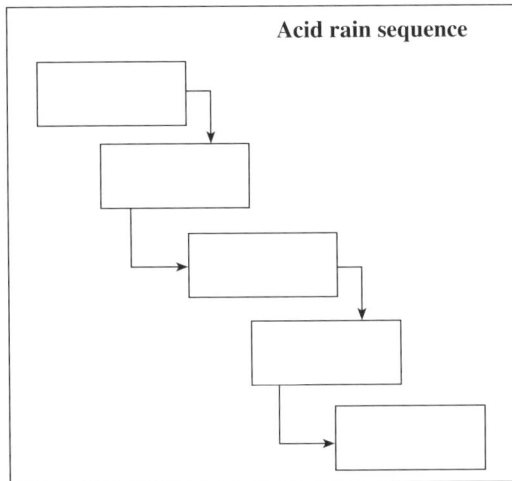

Acid rain sequence

A sulphur dioxide rises into the atmosphere   B acid rain falls
C fish die in acidified lakes   D discarded car batteries leak acid
E fuel combustion in power stations   F ozone is produced in power stations
G pollutant combines with water vapour

4 Householders in the UK produce approximately 20 million tonnes of domestic waste each year.
The table shows the average composition of domestic waste.

Type of waste material	Percentage of total
Paper and board	32
Food and garden rubbish	24
Glass	10
Plastics	7
Metal	4
Other	

a Complete the table, and then draw a bar graph of the information it contains. *(5)*
b What is meant by the term biodegradable?
Give one example of material that is biodegradable. *(3)*
c Much food and garden rubbish is disposed of in plastic bags.
The interior of the bag is anaerobic, and an explosive gas can be formed.
What is the name of this explosive gas? *(1)*
d If the 'other' category is ignored, what percentage of the total domestic waste could be biodegradable?
Show your working. *(3)*

1   The chart shows the number of Orkney voles and short-eared owls on Birsey Moor over a
    period of ten years.

Owl and vole populations

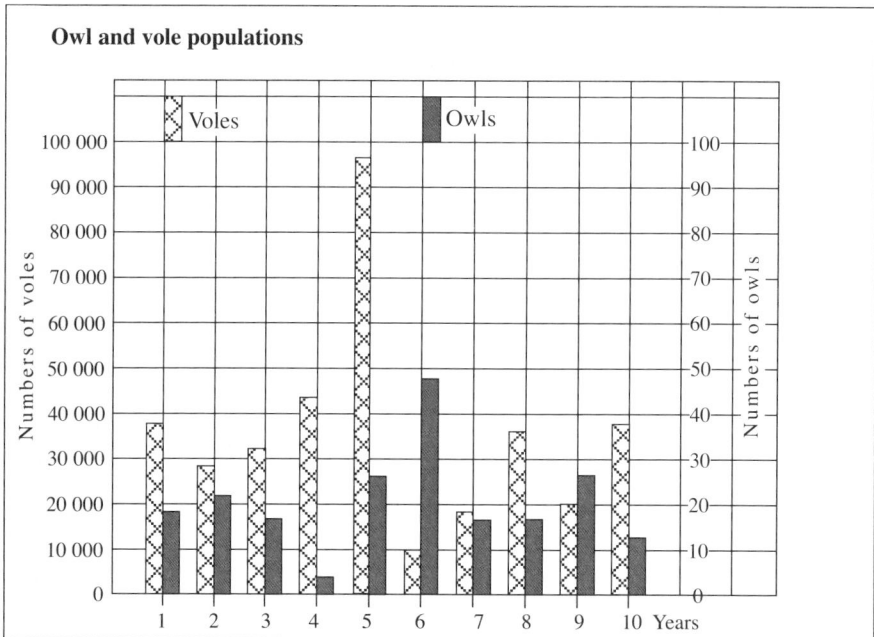

a   How many voles were there in year 3? *(1)*

b   How many owls were there in year 3? *(1)*

c   By how much did the vole population increase between years 4 and 5?
    Give your answer as a percentage and show your working. *(3)*

d   Gamekeepers believed that short-eared owls ate grouse chicks, and so shot as
    many owls as they could during year 4. The gamekeepers supply grain to grouse
    chicks. Voles feed on grain as well as other plant material.
    Using information from the graph, explain whether their plan to kill owls
    would be likely to increase grouse populations. *(4)*

e   Palm oil planters in Malaysia noted that owls were very effective at catching
    rodents such as voles and rats. Rats eat the palm nuts needed to produce the
    oil, so the planters introduced owls to limit the numbers of rats.
    What is the name given to this type of ecological management? *(1)*

f   Why is it important that some rats escape from the owls and continue to breed? *(2)*

2   The Prickly Pear cactus has been a considerable pest in Eastern Australia.
    The plant was introduced as a garden hedge and stock control fence in 1840, but soon
    'escaped' and took over large areas of land. These areas of land could not be cultivated
    because the Prickly Pear grows so quickly. Control methods such as cutting and spraying
    did not work, and the search for a more effective control became a desperate one.

In 1925 a British scientist identified a moth, _Cactoblastis cactorum_, whose caterpillars fed only on Prickly Pear. The caterpillars were produced in large numbers and released into the areas infested with the cactus. The cactus was soon cleared, and the land was available for cultivation once more.

The cactus population increases from time to time, but there are always enough moths to breed quickly and produce a large population of caterpillars.

a The use of moths in this way is an example of Biological Control.
   Apart from being successful, give two advantages of this method over
   chemical control systems. *(2)*

b Give two factors that must be considered when choosing one organism to
   control another species in this way. *(2)*

c Why is it important that the caterpillar does not destroy all of the cacti? *(2)*

d Draw a graph relating the population of a pest, such as the cactus, to its
   control agent, such as the caterpillar. *(4)*

e Greenfly (a type of aphid) can be a serious pest in greenhouses, and can
   reduce tomato crops by more than 50%.
   i   Why are greenfly such a serious pest to tomatoes? *(2)*
   ii Describe a biological control system that has been used on greenfly. *(2)*

3 The table lists some advantages of biological pest control, compared with
   chemical pest control.
   Complete the first column of the table, choosing terms from the list that follows. *(5)*

A specificity   B accumulation in ecosystems

C permanence of control   D development of pest resistance

E cost in financial terms

Factor	Biological control	Chemical control
	Very high, so little danger to humans or beneficial species	May be low, but legislation leading to great improvements
	Initially may be high, but very low in the long term	May be very high, restricting use to wealthy nations
	Very rare	Common, requiring ever-increasing doses
	Good, but small numbers of pests must be tolerated	Requires regular reapplication
	None	Concentrations may increase along food chains

PHOTOSYNTHESIS AND PLANT NUTRITION

1   The diagram shows a section through part of a leaf.

    a Name the cells labelled A, B, C, D and E *(5)*

    b In which of the cells, A to E, does most photosynthesis occur? *(1)*

    c Which of these cells, A to E transport water and minerals to the leaf? *(1)*

    d In what form is carbohydrate transported around the plant? *(1)*

    e i In what form is carbohydrate stored in an onion? *(1)*

      ii Describe how you would carry out a test for this storage carbohydrate. Describe a positive result. *(2)*

      iii Describe two uses, other than storage, for the carbohydrate made by the process of photosynthesis. *(2)*

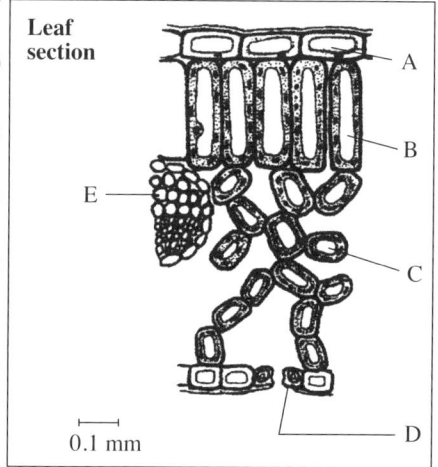

Leaf section — A, B, C, D, E — 0.1 mm

    f Look back at the leaf section.
Use the scale to work out:

      i the thickness of the leaf

      ii the length of a palisade cell

    Show your working. *(2)*

2   The diagram shows the movement of materials in and out of a leaf during photosynthesis.

    a Name the gas entering the leaf at A. *(1)*

    b Name the gas entering the atmosphere at B. *(1)*

    c Which raw material, required for photosynthesis, enters the leaf at C? *(1)*

    d Which mineral, required for the synthesis of proteins, enters the leaf at C? *(1)*

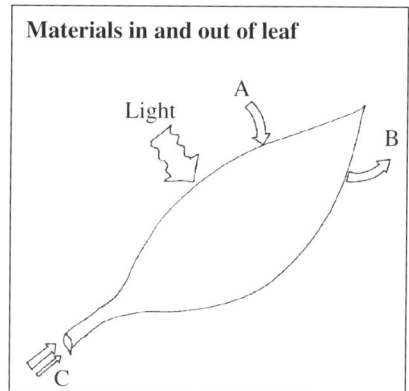

Materials in and out of leaf — Light, A, B, C

The graph on the next page shows the variation in carbon dioxide concentration in the atmosphere close to a daffodil plant over a 24 hour period.

Graph of CO$_2$ changes

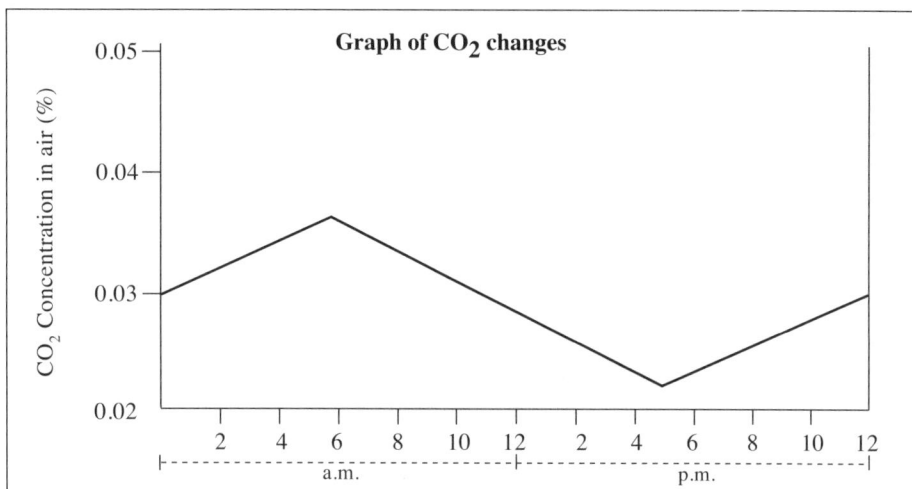

e Name the process in the daffodil cells that caused the change in CO$_2$
   concentration between 8 a.m. and 12 a.m. *(1)*

f Write out a word equation for this process. *(2)*

g Apart from carbon dioxide concentration what environmental factor has the
   greatest effect on the rate of photosynthesis during the 24 hour period? *(1)*

h Explain how animals benefit from the process of photosynthesis. *(2)*

3 Some plants have variegated leaves - (some parts of the leaf are green and other parts are
   white). A plant of this type was placed in a dark cupboard for 48 hours. When it was
   removed it had part of one leaf covered with black paper and then it was left exposed to
   bright light. After six hours, small discs were cut from the leaf and each was tested for
   the presence of starch. The experiment is summarised in the diagram below:

a What was the reason for placing the
   plant in the darkened cupboard? *(2)*

b Describe the test used for the presence
   of starch. List the steps carefully.
   Use a diagram in your answer. *(4)*

c Name the mineral ion necessary for the
   synthesis of the green pigment in
   the leaves. *(1)*

d Use the results of the experiment to
   name one factor necessary for
   photosynthesis.
   Explain why this factor is necessary
   for the process. *(2)*

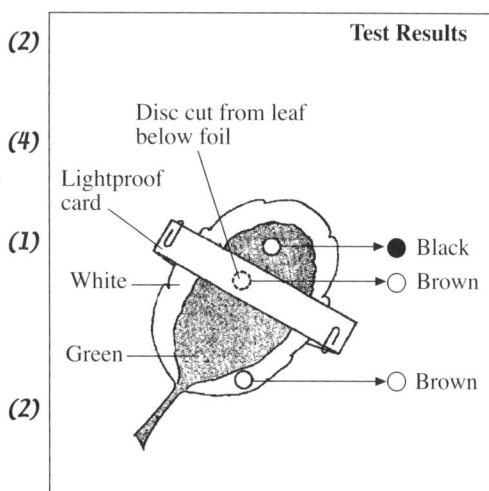

Test Results

Disc cut from leaf
below foil

Lightproof
card

White

Green

● Black
○ Brown
○ Brown

1   Use words from the following list to complete the paragraphs below.

phloem, vascular, active transport, osmosis, diffusion, respiration, xylem, surface area,
nitrate, ions, solvent, photosynthesis, digestion, support, hairs, epidermis, magnesium

Water is obtained by plants from the soil solution. The water enters by the process of
......................., via special structures on the outside of the root called root ....
These structures increase the .... of the root and, as well as absorbing water,
they can also take up .... such as ....which is required for the
synthesis of chlorophyll. These substances are absorbed both by .... and by
.... , a process that requires the supply of energy.

Plant cells rely on water for ...., as a .... and as a raw material
for .... Water is used as a transport medium for both ions and
sugars. The ions are transported, along with water, in the .... tissue. Sugars
are transported through living cells of the .... these specialised tissues are
grouped together into .... bundles.   *(13)*

2   Using the apparatus shown below, a student set out to investigate the factors which
influence water uptake by a plant.

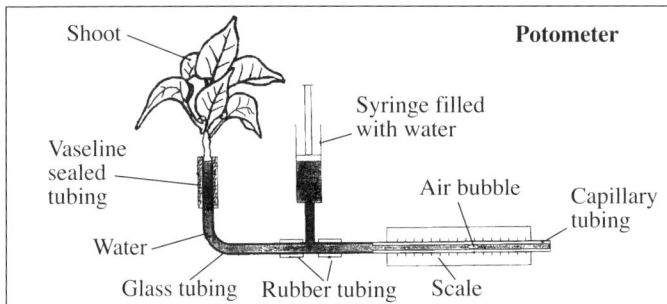

After a series of experiments he obtained the following results:

Environmental condition	Time taken for bubble to move 10 cm/ min	Rate of bubble movement /cm per minute
1 High light intensity	4	
2 High humidity(plant enclosed in clear plastic bag)	17	
3 Wind (electric fan blowing over plant surface)	1.5	
4 Dark and windy	19	
5 Dark and low humidity	22	

a Calculate the rate at which the bubble moves. *(5)*

Plot these results in the form of a bar chart. *(5)*

b Plants require light for photosynthesis, and 'anticipate' the need for carbon dioxide uptake during photosynthesis by opening their stomata under appropriate conditions. Does this help to explain the results of the first experiment? Explain your answer. *(2)*

c Water is lost from leaves by evaporation and diffusion if the stomata are open, and a suitable water potential gradient exists.

Use this information to explain the results of experiments 2 and 5. *(3)*

d How can you explain the results of experiments 3 and 4? *(2)*

3 Examine the diagram shown below. Identify the tissues labelled A, B and C on Diagram A. *(3)*

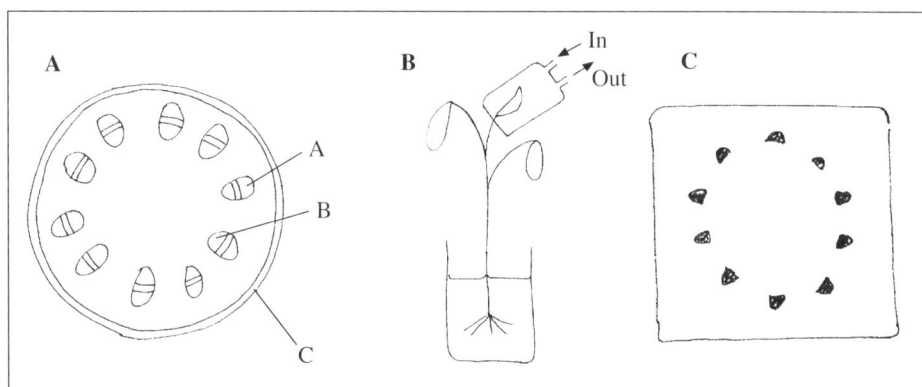

An experiment was carried out using the plant shown in diagram B. The roots of the plant were allowed to stand in a solution of eosin (a red-coloured dye), and one of the leaves was kept inside a container that could be filled with radioactively-labelled carbon dioxide. The apparatus was placed in bright light for 6 hours. A cross-section of the stem was then cut using a sharp scalpel.

a Which of the tissues A, B or C would be stained red?
Explain your answer. *(2)*

b The section was allowed to stand on a piece of film sensitive to radiation.
When the film was developed it appeared as shown in Diagram C.
Explain why it appeared like this.

4 Which of the following comparisons is not correct? Explain your answer. *(2)*

	Desert plant	Woodland plant
A	more resistant to drought	Less resistant to drought
B	Leaves often fleshy	Leaves often thin and rolled
C	Root system is deeper than normal	Root system shallower than desert plant
D	Leaves often rolled up	Leaves rarely rolled up
E	Leaf system small in comparison with root system	Leaf system usually large in comparison with root system

1 All living organisms respond to changes in their environment. The responses they show have an important effect on their survival. Plants respond by altering their direction of growth. Because growth is involved, plants respond more slowly than animals do.

Complete the following sentences about plant responses.

a A tropism is defined as a change in the direction of .... of a plant in response to a directional ....

b In geotropism, the plant is responding to ....

c The shoot of a plant will grow towards light, that is it shows ....
phototropism. This response allows the plant to produce more food by .... *(5)*

2 Growing oat seedlings are placed in a box that only allows light from one side to reach them, as shown in the diagram below.

Which of the following conclusions is the correct one. Explain your answer. *(2)*

The shoot with the tinfoil cap ...

A cannot photosynthesise without light, and so cannot grow in a curved shape

B is too far away from the light to be stimulated

C cannot respond because the tips must receive the stimulus

D is deprived of carbon dioxide, and so cannot grow

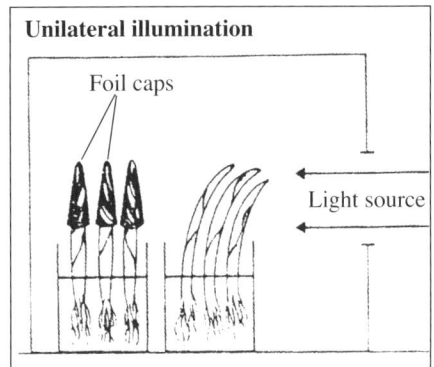

Unilateral illumination

Foil caps

Light source

3 Study the diagram, which shows a rush plant growing at the edge of a lake.

a What is the name of the growth response shown by the young shoot? *(1)*

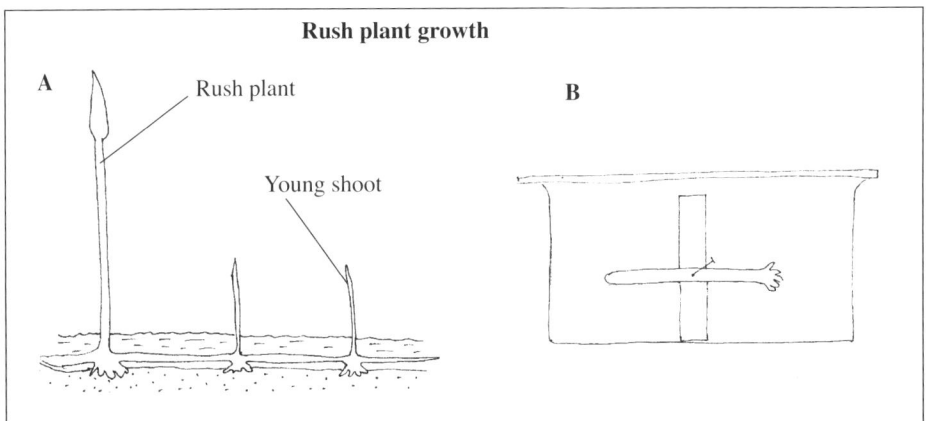

Rush plant growth

A Rush plant

B

Young shoot

b What is the name of the growth response shown by the roots of the rush plants? What survival advantage does this growth response give to the rush plants? *(2)*

c Figure B shows a single young plant pinned out horizontally inside a clear plastic box. Light shines on the box from directly above it.
Draw the young plant as it would appear 24 hours later. *(2)*

4 Young oat seedlings were treated with a substance X. The substance X was given to the seedling by mixing it with lanolin paste and smearing the paste on one side of the seedling, as shown in the diagram.

An experiment was carried out in which different concentrations of substance X were given to different seedlings, and the angle A measured in each case. The results are shown below:

Concentration of X (mg per dm³)	Angle A (degrees)
1	3
2	6
4	10
7	16
10	19

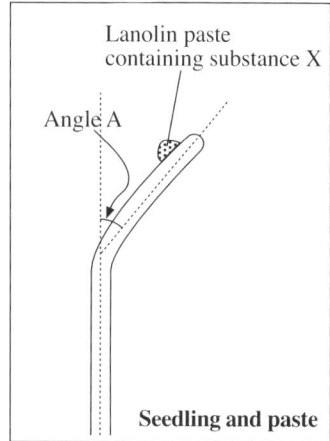

Lanolin paste containing substance X

Angle A

Seedling and paste

a Plot these results in the form of a graph. *(5)*
b What would be the value of angle A at a concentration of X of 5 mg per dm³? *(2)*
c What is the name given to the response shown by the oat seedlings? *(1)*
d What is the name of substance X? *(1)*

5 Plant hormones affect many aspects of plant growth.
Suggest three ways in which a farmer could use plant hormones. *(3)*

6 The diagram shows a section through half of a broad bean seed.

a Name all of the parts labelled A – E on the diagram. *(5)*
b Structure B contains a food store.
A teacher explained that the food store provided energy for the growing seed.
One student thought that the food would be fat, and another thought that it would be carbohydrate.
Describe a test that you could carry out to decide who was right (or whether both were!). Name the reagents that you would use, the steps you would take and the results you might expect. *(5)*

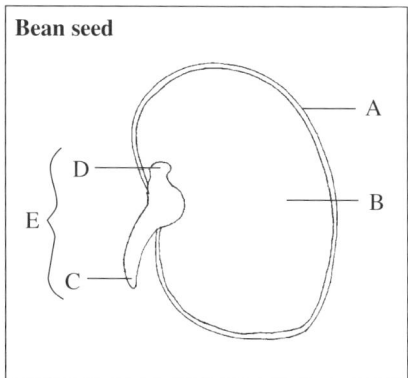

Bean seed

A

D

B

E

C

4 - THE WORLD OF ANIMALS

TRANSPORT IN ANIMALS

1   The table shows the cell composition of three samples of blood.

	Jack	James	Julian
Red cells/ number per mm³	8 200 000	5 000 000	2 200 000
White cells/ number per mm³	500	8 000	5 000
Platelets/ number per mm³	280 000	255 000	1 000

   a Which person is most likely to have recently lived at high altitude?
      Explain your answer.   *(2)*

   b Which person would be least likely to resist infection by a virus?
      Explain your answer.   *(2)*

   c People at risk from heart disease are sometimes recommended to take half
      an aspirin each day. Aspirin reduces the clotting of blood, so prevents blood
      clots blocking narrowed arteries.
      Which person is most likely to be taking this drug each day? Explain your answer. *(2)*

   d Iron deficiency in the diet can cause a condition called anaemia.
      Which person is likely to show the symptoms of anaemia? Explain your answer. *(2)*

   e These three samples were all taken from 25-year-old men.
      Explain why this makes comparisons between them more valid. *(2)*

2   Study the following diagram (taken from the notes of a medical student) carefully,
then answer the questions based on it.

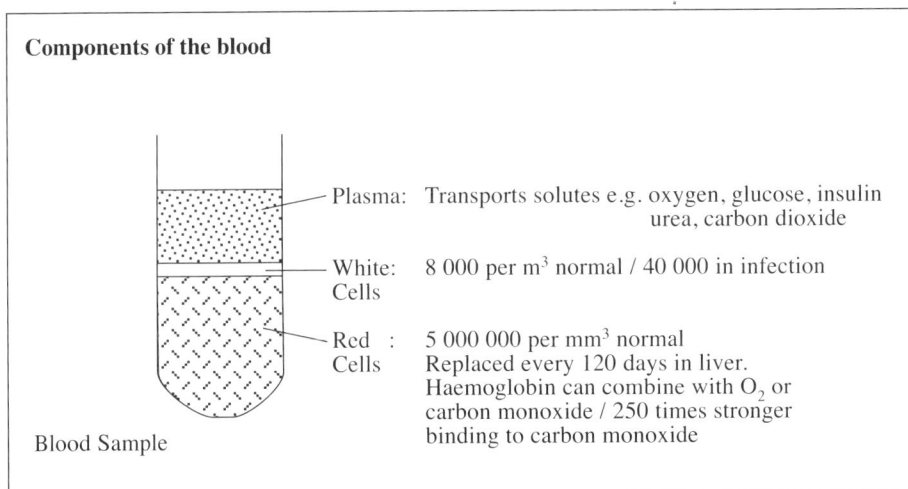

Components of the blood

Plasma: Transports solutes e.g. oxygen, glucose, insulin
urea, carbon dioxide

White: 8 000 per m³ normal / 40 000 in infection
Cells

Red : 5 000 000 per mm³ normal
Cells Replaced every 120 days in liver.
Haemoglobin can combine with O_2 or
carbon monoxide / 250 times stronger
binding to carbon monoxide

Blood Sample

   a Name two soluble substances transported in the blood plasma.
      For each substance you name, suggest where it might be coming from and
      where it might be going.   *(2)*

b What is the maximum number of white blood cells normally found in 1 mm³ of blood. What can cause this number to increase? *(2)*

c In a healthy person what is the ratio of red cells to white cells? *(1)*

d What happens to the amount of oxygen transported in a person who smokes regularly. Explain your answer. *(2)*

e How long would it take the blood of the person noted in part **d** to regain its full ability to carry oxygen? Explain your answer. *(3)*

3 Study the diagram below. This diagram shows a ventral (front) view of a human heart, and the main blood vessels attached to it.

a Name the blood vessels labelled A and B. *(2)*

b Which organ will be at the end of the blood vessel labelled C? *(1)*

c Complete the sentence about the blood inside vessel D.
The blood is at … (low/high) ………
pressure, is …(purple/red)…..in colour
and has a … (low/high) ……….
concentration of oxygen. *(3)*

d Explain how the structures labelled E help to keep blood flowing in one direction only. *(2)*

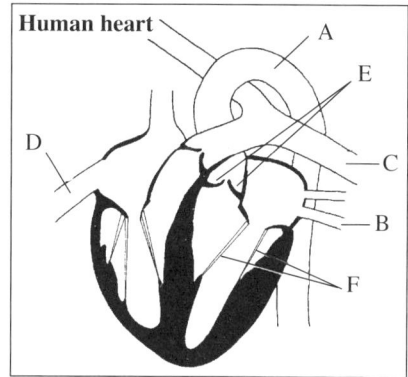

Human heart

e What is the function of the structures labelled F? *(2)*

4 The diagram shows three types of blood vessel in the human circulation.

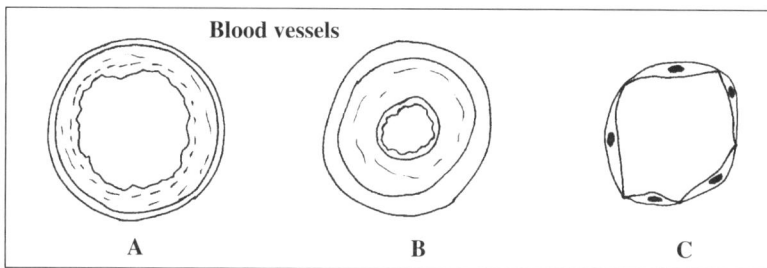

Blood vessels

A   B   C

Use the label letters (A, B or C) to identify the vessels that

a have walls one cell thick *(1)*
b allow amino acids to cross the walls *(1)*
c have valves to prevent back-flow *(1)*
d carry blood to the heart *(1)*
e carry blood under high pressure *(1)*
f pulse as blood flows through them *(1)*
g can be blocked by fatty tissue called atheroma *(1)*
h carry blood away from the heart *(1)*
i have thick elastic walls *(1)*
j increase greatly in number after long periods of athletic training. *(1)*

1   Match up the two lists below to explain the ideal features of a gas exchange surface.   *(5)*

	Feature		Value in gas exchange
A	moist	a.	gases do not have to diffuse very far
B	large surface area	b	oxygen is quickly removed so that diffusion can continue
C	thin	c	increase the number of molecules that can diffuse across at the same time
D	well ventilated	d	cells die if they dry out
E	good blood supply	e	regular supply of fresh air keeps up the concentration gradients for oxygen and carbon dioxide

2   Complete the following paragraph by filling in the missing words.
    The words in the following list may be used once, more than once, or not at all.

energy, hydrogencarbonate, left atrium, pulmonary, respiration, thin, oxygen, surface area, renal, alveoli, capillaries, arteries, trachea, right ventricle.

Deoxygenated blood arrives at the lungs in the ....arteries. Oxygen has been removed from the blood by cells that are carrying out .... to release .... needed to carry out their functions. This blood also contains a relatively high concentration of the gas .... , which is carried dissolved in the plasma as .... ions. Each artery branches many times to form ...., which are well adapted to allow the exchange of gases because they are .... -walled and have a very large .... These small vessels lie very close to the .... of the lungs, and it is here that gas exchange takes place. The gas .... moves out of the blood and the gas ....moves into the blood. Both gases move by the process of .... Oxygenated blood then leaves the lungs in the .... vein that returns blood to the heart at the chamber called the ....   *(14)*

3   Complete the following paragraphs. The words in the following list may be used once, more than once, or not at all.

gills, oxygen, energy, thin, Amoeba, nitrogen, moist, spiracles, respiration, excretion, surface area, blood, tracheoles, ventilation, carbon dioxide

All living organisms require .... which is released from the process of .... The most efficient form of this process requires the gas .... and produces the waste gas .... To keep this energy-releasing process going the organism must have a gas exchange surface – this surface has certain properties.

These have a large ...., a .... membrane so that diffusion distances are short and a .... layer (since cells die if they dry out). In addition the most advanced systems have a means of .... to move the gases over the surface, and are close to a .... supply to transport gases between the surface and the living tissues.

In simple organisms such as .... enough oxygen can diffuse through the outer cell membrane, but larger organisms require more oxygen than diffusion alone can supply. Insects have small 'holes', called .... , in their body covering – these connect to tubes called .... that lead directly to the working tissues. More active and larger animals may have a specialised gas exchange surface , such as the .... found in fish. *(13)*

4   Study the diagram below. This represents the human respiratory system.

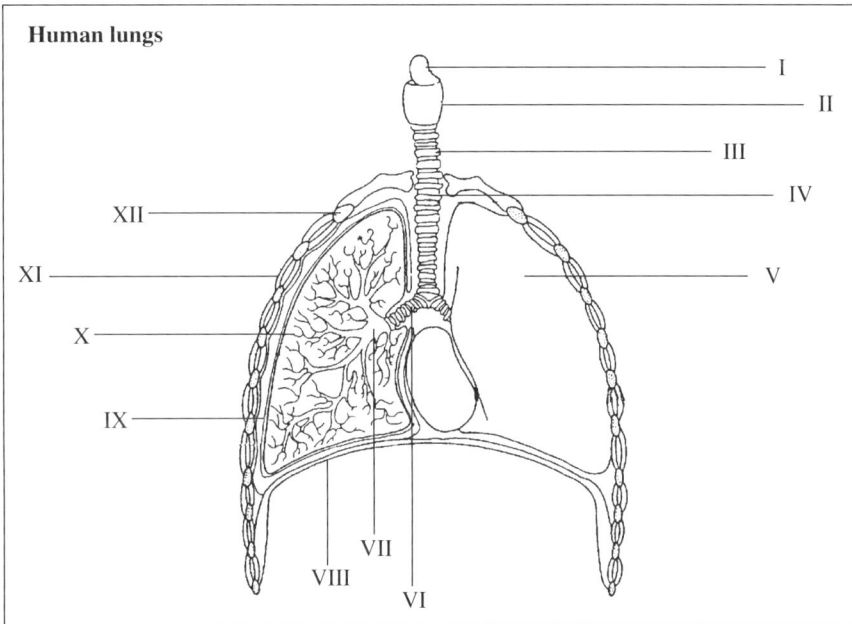

Human lungs

Which of the structures labelled I – XII:

a helps to keep the air passages open
b move the rib cage during breathing
c form a cage to protect the heart and lungs from physical damage
d separates the thorax from the abdomen, to make breathing more efficient
e make sure that the lungs follow the ribs during breathing in
f is the place where sounds are produced
g is the actual site of gas exchange
h is also known as the 'windpipe'? *(8)*

1 The diagram below shows the human alimentary canal.

Human alimentary canal

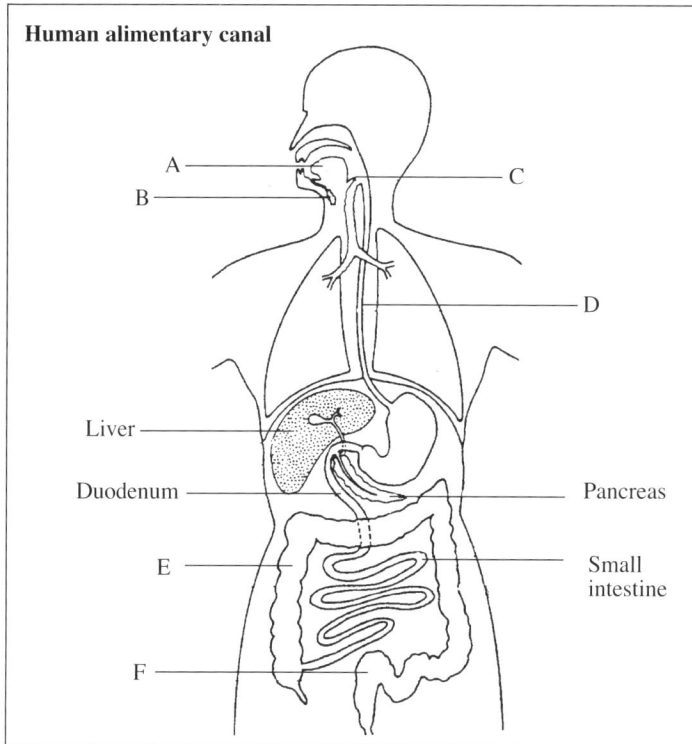

a Name the part labelled A. *(1)*
b Explain how A and B work together to make swallowing more efficient. *(2)*
c Why is C important when swallowing? *(1)*
d Draw a labelled diagram to explain how food is moved along the structure D. *(2)*
e Describe two features of the small intestine which help to increase its surface area. *(2)*
f The liver has many functions, including the storage of excess carbohydrate.
  i Name the carbohydrate used to store excess sugar in the liver. *(1)*
  ii Name the blood vessel that carries sugar from the intestine to the liver *(1)*
  iii Name the blood vessel that carries glucose released from the liver some time after feeding. *(1)*
  iv The liver also produces bile. What is the function of bile? Where does bile have its effect? *(2)*
g The pancreas produces enzymes and releases them into the duodenum.
  i How do the enzymes produced in the pancreas get into the duodenum? *(1)*
  ii Name one enzyme produced by the pancreas. State what kind of foodstuff it works on, and what the products are. *(3)*
h Give one function of each of the parts labelled E and F. *(2)*

2   The table shows the composition and energy content of four common foods.

Food	Energy content (kJ per g)	Composition per 100g					
		Protein (g)	Fat (g)	Carbohydrate (g)	Vitamin C (mg)	Vitamin D (mg)	Iron (mg)
A	3700	0.5	80	0	0	40	0
B	150	1.2	0.6	7	200	0	0
C	400	2.0	0.2	25	10	0	8
D	1200	9.0	1.5	60	0	0	0

a   Which food would be best to prevent rickets?
b   Which food would be best for a young man training for cross-country running?
c   Which food would be most needed by a menstruating woman?
d   Which food would be the most useful to a body-builder?
e   Which food would be most dangerous for a person with heart disease?   *(5)*

3   Lengths of Visking tubing were set up as shown in the diagram

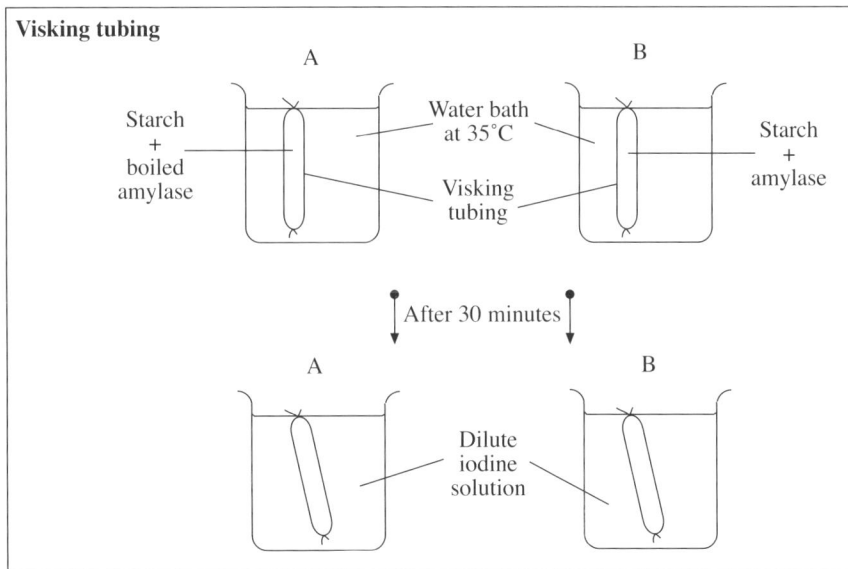

Tube A contained starch and boiled amylase solution
Tube B contained starch and amylase.
Both tubes were left in a water bath at 35°C for 30 minutes. The tubes were then removed from the water baths, gently blotted with paper towels, and then placed in beakers of dilute iodine solution for five minutes. Visking tubing is permeable to iodine solution.

a   What colour would you expect to see inside **i** A   and   **ii** B?   *(2)*
b   Explain why the results are different for tubing A and B.   *(2)*
c   Describe a test you could use to prove your explanation.   *(3)*

35

1 The diagram shows a single neuron.

Which of the parts, labelled A – F …

a connects with another neuron
b insulates the axon to limit interference with other neurones
c contains high concentrations of chemicals called neurotransmitters
d connects with an effector, such as a muscle
e allows a nerve impulse to 'jump' quickly along the axon
f contains DNA?   *(6 x 1)*

Neuron

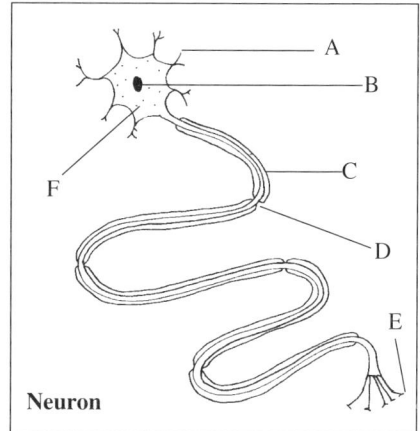

2 The diagram shows a section through an eye.

Which of the parts labelled A – F …

a contains rods and cones
b is black to prevent internal reflection of light
c is a muscle controlling the amount of light entering the eye
d contains neurones leading to the visual centre in the brain
e is tough enough to act as an attachment for the muscles that move the eye in its socket
f helps to converge light towards the retina?   *(6 x 1)*

Eye section

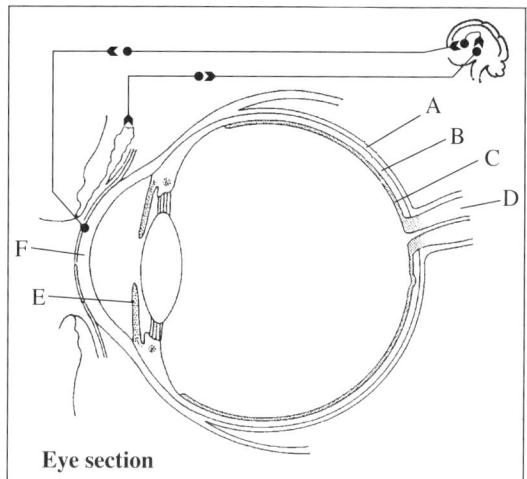

The diagram above also shows the pathway of an important reflex involved in protection of the eye.

g complete and rearrange the boxes to show that you understand the pathway of this action   *(5)*

| Effector is … |

| Stimulus is … |

| Receptor is … |

| Coordinator is … |

| Response is … |

h what is the survival value of this reflex?   *(1)*

3   The bar graph shows the units of alcohol present in some different types of alcoholic
    drink. The line graph relates alcohol level in the blood to the units of alcohol consumed.

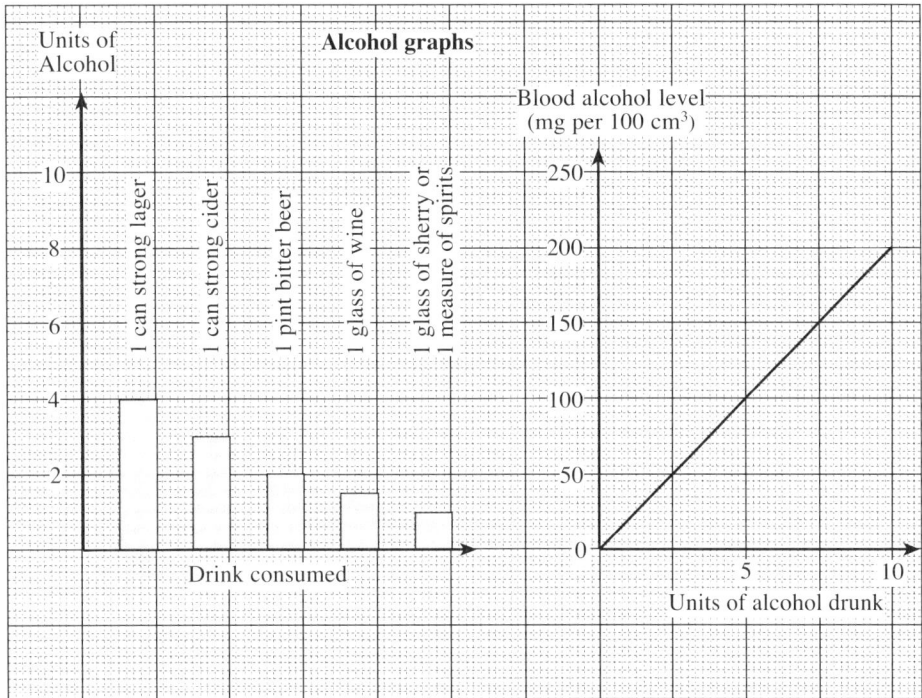

   a How many units of alcohol are present in one can of strong lager?   *(1)*
   b How much alcohol would be present in the blood after drinking a pint of
      bitter and two measures of whisky?   *(2)*
   c The UK limit for blood alcohol level in a person driving a car is 80mg per 100 cm³.
      A person drank three cans of cider and one glass of wine - by how much
      would her blood alcohol level be over the legal limit? Show your working.   *(3)*
   d Why is it dangerous to drive when over the 'legal limit'?   *(2)*
   e Alcohol is cleared from the bloodstream by the action of the liver, at the rate
      of about 1 unit per hour. How many hours after drinking the alcohol described
      in part **c** would a person 'safe' to drive?   *(2)*
   f Name the disease of the liver caused by excessive consumption of alcohol.   *(1)*

4   Complete the paragraph by filling in the gaps with words from the list below.
    You may use each word once, more than once, or not at all.   *(6)*

*adrenaline, hormone, bloodstream, digestive system, endocrine organ, insulin, target
organ, trachea, oesophagus*

In all mammals there is a chemical coordination system. This system uses chemical
messengers called ...., which are secreted by the ...., travel in
the .... and have an effect on a .... An example of this type
of chemical messenger is .... which, during periods of fear or anxiety,
relaxes the ....allowing the person to breathe more easily.

1 The diagram shows the position of the excretory system in a human.

Use the letters A – G to identify the following structures that …

a carry urine out of the body.
b deliver blood with a high urea content.
c carry urine away from the kidney.
d filter urea and other wastes from the blood.
e store urine until it is convenient to expel it.
f remain contracted until a nervous message instructs it to relax. **(6 x 1)**

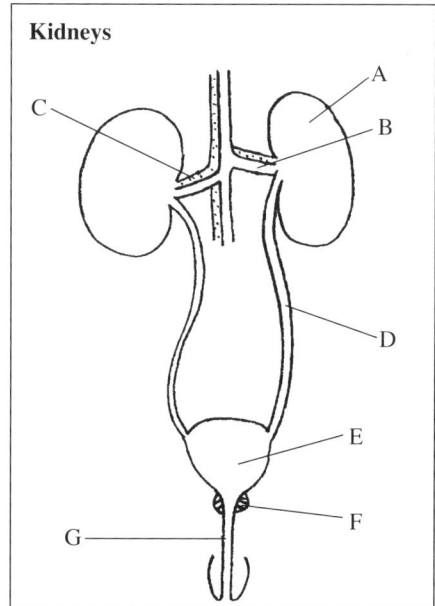

Kidneys

2 The graph shows the changes in urine production and ADH secretion following a drink of 500 cm³ of water.

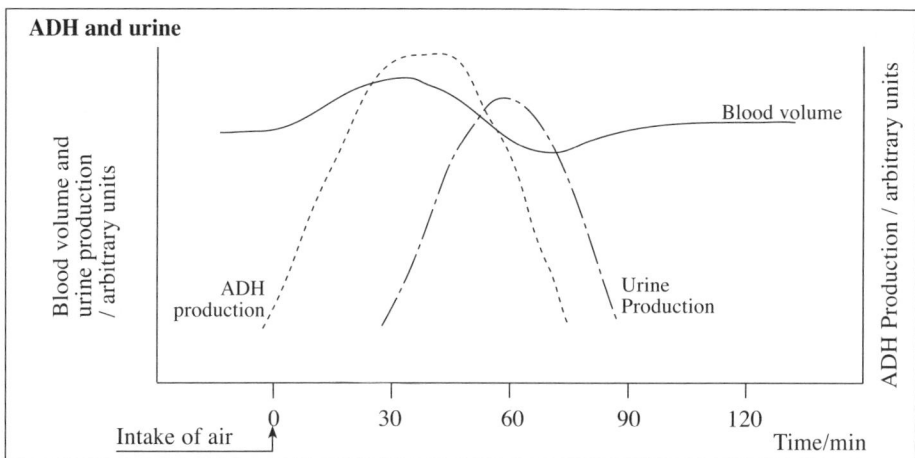

ADH and urine

Blood volume and urine production / arbitrary units

ADH Production / arbitrary units

Blood volume

ADH production

Urine Production

Intake of air

0   30   60   90   120

Time/min

a What do the initials ADH stand for? *(1)*
b Once a stimulus is received, how long does it take the pituitary gland to reach 50% of its maximum ADH output? *(1)*
c Explain how the graph can be used to illustrate the principle of negative feedback. *(3)*

3   The diagram shows part of an artificial kidney machine.

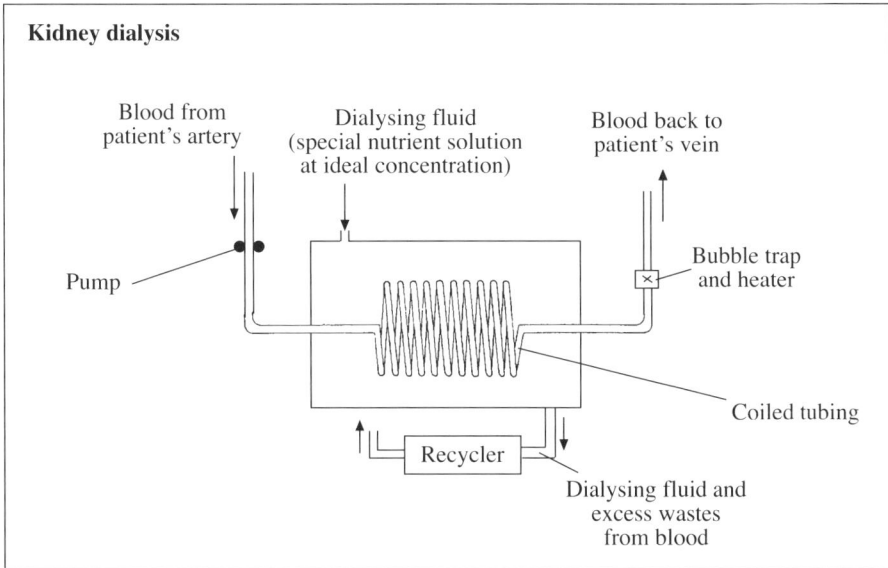

Kidney dialysis

Blood from patient's artery

Dialysing fluid (special nutrient solution at ideal concentration)

Blood back to patient's vein

Pump

Bubble trap and heater

Coiled tubing

Recycler

Dialysing fluid and excess wastes from blood

a   What is the advantage of using coiled tubing in the machine? *(1)*
b   What is the name of the process that allows urea from the blood to pass into the dialysis fluid? *(1)*
c   Suggest *two* very important features of the dialysis tubing. Explain your answers. *(2)*
d   Why is the blood passed through a heater before returning it to the patient's vein? *(1)*
e   The recycler treats the dialysis fluid with an enzyme called urease. Give one reason why this enzyme is used. *(1)*
f   Give three reasons why a kidney transplant is a better way to treat kidney disease than the use of a dialysis machine. *(3)*
g   What are the two main problems facing the successful treatment of kidney disease with a transplant programme. *(2)*

4   The diagram shows a section through human skin.

a   Identify the structures labelled A, B, C, D and E. *(5)*
b   Explain how structures A and D are involved in cooling an overheated body. *(3)*
c   Explain how structures A, B and C are involved in the response to falling temperature. *(3)*
d   The polar bear has a much deeper layer E towards the end of the summer. Why? *(2)*

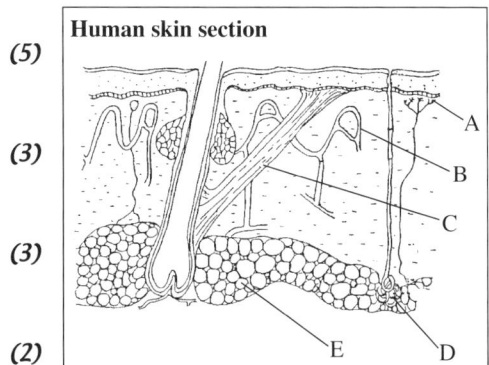

Human skin section

A

B

C

E

D

5 - Variation and Inheritance

Cell division

1   a   What is a chromosome?   *(1)*
    b   How many chromosomes are there in
        i   A skin cell from a human male
        ii   A human egg cell
        iii   A red blood cell from a human female
        iv   A red blood cell from a human male?   *(4 x 1)*
    c   Name the process in which haploid cells are formed from diploid cells.   *(1)*
    d   Name the process which provides new cells for the growth of a young mammal.   *(1)*

2   This diagram represents the life cycle of a mammal.

    a   Copy and complete the diagram by writing in the
        circles the numbers of chromosomes found in the
        nuclei of these cells if the mammal concerned was
        a human.   *(5)*
    b   In what way is this diagram misleading?   *(1)*
    c   Where, exactly, does meiosis occur in a mammal? *(1)*
    d   Why is it necessary for gametes to be formed
        by meiosis?   *(2)*

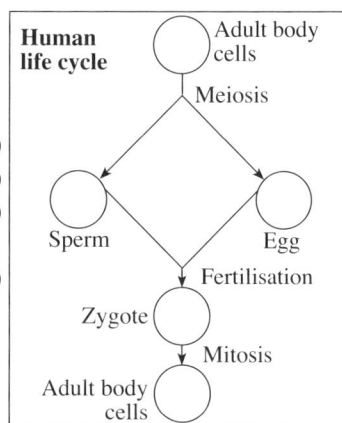

3   The diagram below shows the sex chromosomes in a human couple.

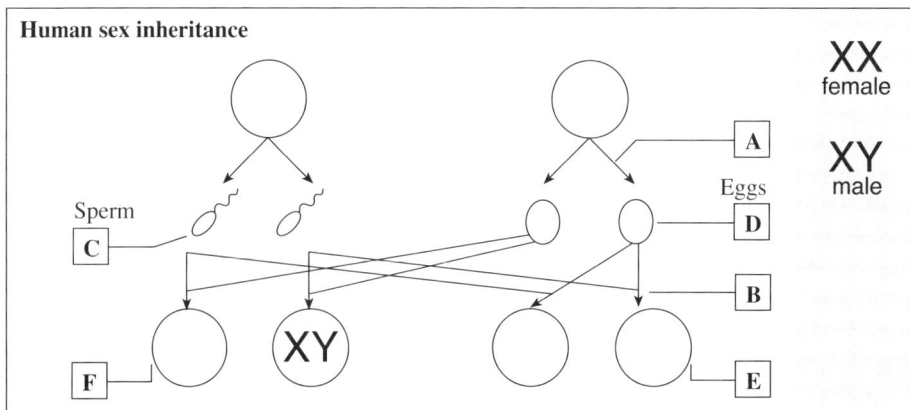

    a   Identify the two processes labelled A and B.   *(2)*
    b   Write out the sex chromosomes present in the cells labelled C, D, E and F.   *(4)*
    c   If a couple have three children, two boys (aged 7 and 5) and a girl (aged 2),
        what is the probability that the next child will be a girl? Explain your answer.   *(2)*

4 Chromosomes can be extracted from cells floating in the amniotic fluid that surrounds a developing baby. These chromosomes can be studied by scientists – for example they can provide information about the sex of the developing child. These diagrams show the chromosomes of two different children.

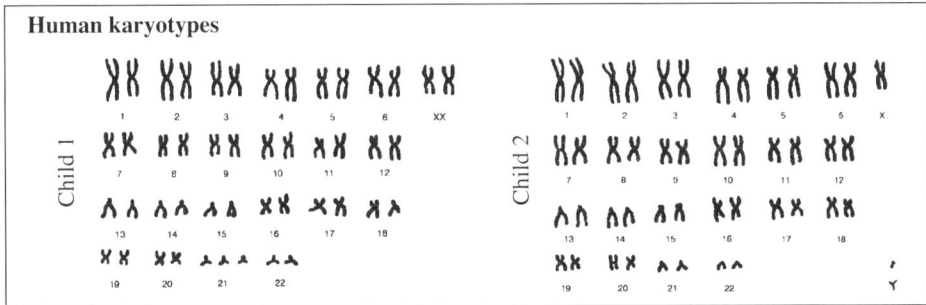

Human karyotypes

a Identify two differences between the chromosome set of Child I and Child II. *(2)*
b One child has an abnormal set of chromosomes. Which child is it? *(1)*
c What is the name of the condition caused by this set of chromosomes? *(1)*

5 It is possible to observe the process of mitosis in cells which are actively dividing. The tips of roots and shoots have many dividing cells when a plant is increasing in length.

A student was able to cut off the top 5 mm of a plant shoot. She then softened it by warming it in a dilute solution of hydrochloric acid, and squashed the tip onto a microscope slide. The squashed cells were treated with a red dye, and then observed under a light microscope.

a Why did she soften the tip? *(1)*
b Why did she squash the tip? *(1)*
c Why is red dye added to the preparation? *(1)*
d The student took some photographs of the dividing cells.
These are shown in these figures.
What would be the sequence of these cells as they divided? *(4)*

e Make a labelled drawing of one chromosome from Figure A. *(2)*
f How many chromatids are present in Figure B? *(1)*
g How many chromosomes would be present in a body cell from this organism? *(1)*

Dividing cells

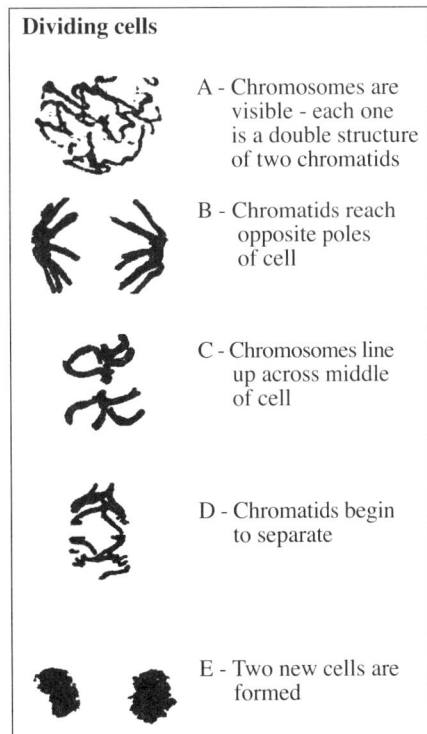

A - Chromosomes are visible - each one is a double structure of two chromatids

B - Chromatids reach opposite poles of cell

C - Chromosomes line up across middle of cell

D - Chromatids begin to separate

E - Two new cells are formed

1 Complete the following paragraphs. Use words and phrases from the following list. You may use each word once, more than once or not at all. *(16)*

genes, effects of environment, phenotype, discontinuous, continuous, natural selection, evolution, blood grouping, environmental, atmospheric, genotype, body mass, nutrients.

Variation occurs in two forms - the first is .... which shows clear cut separation between groups showing this variation (..........................., for example). The second is .... in which there are many intermediate forms between the extremes of the characteristic. A clear example of this second type is ....

.... is the result of ....alone, whilst .... is also affected by ....factors. The sum of the genes that an organism contains is called its .... and the total of all its observable and measurable characteristics is called the .... The two are related in a simple equation .... equals ....plus ....

Variation provides the raw material for .... Organisms may gain an advantage in the struggle for existence, and .... can 'pick out' the organisms with such an advantage. These organisms may then reproduce and pass on their .... to their offspring.

2 Two students in the first year of secondary school were carrying out a mathematical investigation. They decided to measure the masses of all of the other pupils in their class - the results are presented in the table below:

Mass category/kg	Number in category
35-38	1
39-42	2
43-46	4
47-50	6
51-54	9
55-58	4
59-62	1

    a Plot these results as a bar chart. *(5)*
    b Does this illustrate continuous or discontinuous variation? Explain your answer. *(3)*
    c Suggest one characteristic that the students could have recorded which would have illustrated the other kind of variation. *(1)*

3 The Everglades is an enormous flooded area in southern Florida. There are many animals and plants there, and they are well adapted to their environment. The animals and plants have become well adapted by the process of natural selection.

    a The following are stages in the evolution of species by means of natural selection. Rearrange them into the correct sequence.

       A   Survival of the fittest

B   Over-production of offspring
C   Competition causes a struggle for existence
D   Advantageous characteristics are passed on to the offspring
E   Variation occurs between members of the same population   *(5)*

Some of the early European explorers in Florida noticed that there were many types of bird. The following diagram shows the heads of some of these birds:

Heads of birds

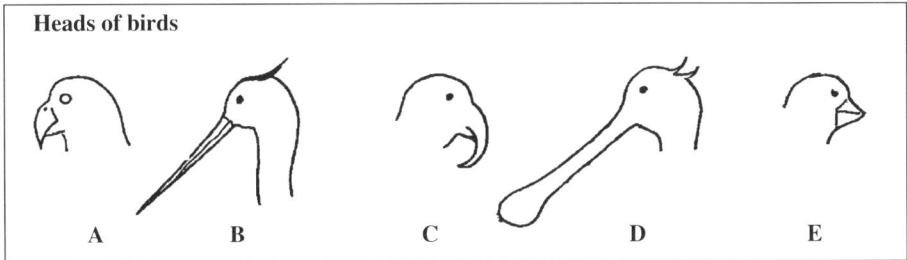

| A | B | C | D | E |

Which type of bird:

b feeds by spearing fish and frogs
c eats snails after extracting them from their shells
d filters algae and small organisms from mud and water
e captures Florida rabbits and other mammals
f feeds on nuts and other hard fruits?   *(5)*

4 The diagram shows a plant that is well adapted to life in a particular environment.

a To what type of environment is this plant suited? Explain your answer.   *(2)*
b Describe three features that suit the plant to its environment.   *(3)*
c Match the letters and the numbers to explain how the mammal shown below is well adapted to its environment.   *(6)*

Cactus

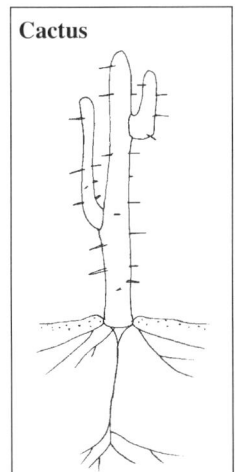

Camel

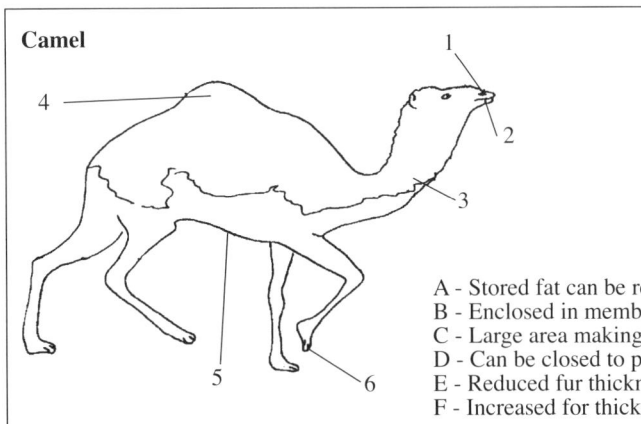

A - Stored fat can be respired to release water
B - Enclosed in membrane to limit evaporation
C - Large area making movement more difficult
D - Can be closed to prevent entry of sand
E - Reduced fur thickness aids heat conduction
F - Increased for thickness limits heat loss

1   The following information can be found in a standard school biology textbook.

Living organisms can pass on their characteristics to the next generation, i.e. they can *reproduce* in two ways:

Asexual Reproduction
*   involves *only one parent organism.*
*   *complete characteristics* of this one parent are passed on to all of the offspring.
*   Many organisms reproduce asexually *when conditions are favorable* (especially when there is much food), and *build up their numbers quickly.*

Sexual Reproduction
*   requires *two organisms of the same species*, one male and one female.
*   Each individual produces special sex cells or *gametes.*
*   Sexual reproduction always involves *fertilisation* i.e. the *fusion of the gametes.*
*   Offspring therefore receive some *genes from each parent*, and thus may show a *mixture of the parental characteristics.*

Which type of reproduction:

a   occurs when an *Amoeba* splits into two   *(1)*
b   is more useful when an organisms has to quickly spread through a particular
    habitat that suits them very well   *(1)*
c   leads to greater variation amongst offspring   *(1)*
d   involves the process of fertilisation   *(1)*
e   requires the production of cells by meiosis?   *(1)*

2   A common garden weed, the Creeping Buttercup, can reproduce asexually by means of runners. The process is summarised in the diagram below.

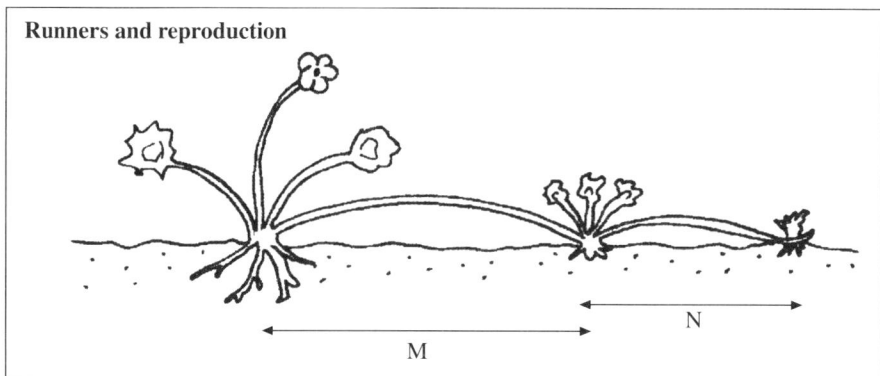

Runners and reproduction

A horticultural student decided to investigate the growth of this weed. He took ten different buttercup plants and measured the lengths of the runners M and N.
The results are shown in the table on the next page:

Plant number	Length of runner M/mm	Length of runner N/mm
1	175	140
2	210	130
3	305	130
4	320	170
5	300	125
6	170	120
7	230	135
8	300	125
9	260	145
10	200	100

a   Calculate the mean lengths for runners M and N. Show your working.   *(4)*
b   Calculate the difference in mean length between runner M and N.   *(2)*
c   Suggest why there are differences between the length M in the ten different plants.   *(2)*
d   The student was trying to develop a weedkiller that could control the buttercups.
    He noticed that one of the plants was very resistant to the weedkiller.
    Explain how this method of reproduction would allow the buttercup to survive
    throughout the garden, even if weedkiller is used.   *(2)*

3   This diagram shows the reproductive system of a human male.

a   Name the parts labelled A, B, C, D and E. *(5)*
b   Identify the part which produces the male
    gametes.   *(1)*
c   Identify the part which produces a liquid
    part of semen.   *(1)*
d   Identify the part which produces
    testosterone.   *(1)*
e   Identify the part which also carries urine.   *(1)*
f   Identify the part which is cut during the
    procedure of vasectomy.   *(1)*

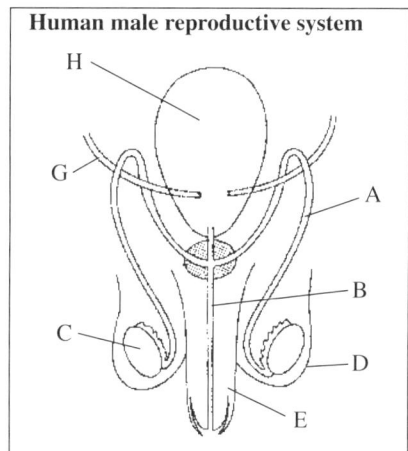

Human male reproductive system

H

G

A

B

C

D

E

4   Arrange the following processes into the correct sequence necessary for the production of
    a human baby.   *(6)*

A - ejaculation

C - birth

B - implantation

D - fertilisation

E - ovulation

F - development

1   Choose words from the following list to match the definitions below.

genotype, allele, Mendel, Darwin, gene, phenotype, heterozygote, dominant, homozygote

   a   The external appearance of an organism
   b   Alternative form of a gene
   c   Studied genetics in Garden Peas
   d   Section of DNA coding for a single characteristic
   e   The set of genes in the nucleus of any individual
   f   A nucleus carrying both alternative alleles of a gene
   g   An allele which determines the appearance of a heterozygote   *(7 x 1)*

2   **a**   Distinguish between the following pairs of terms:

     A - *gene* and *allele*
     B - *homozygous* and *heterozygous*
     C - *phenotype* and *genotype*   *(3 x 2)*

Plum trees are sometimes infected by a fungus. There are some plum trees that are resistant to infection – this resistance is controlled by a recessive allele of a single gene. If a homozygous normal plum tree is crossed with a disease-resistant tree, the resulting F1 plants will contain the allele for resistance. These F1 plants can then be used to produce another disease-resistant crop.

   b   Copy and complete these genetic diagrams to explain how this is possible.   *(2 x 4)*

     Let ..... = allele for normal (disease-sensitive); let .... = allele for disease-resistance.   *(2)*

Inheritance and disease-resistance

    a   Producing F$_1$ plants from homozygous parents

    b   Producing resistant plants from F$_1$ parents

---

3   Cystic fibrosis is one of the most common inherited diseases in Humans.
The disease is caused by the inheritance of a recessive allele – about 1 in 20 white-skinned individuals are heterozygous for this allele. Heterozygotes do not show symptoms of the disease, but are 'carriers' of the allele.

   a   Copy and complete the genetic diagram on the next page to show the possible inheritance of cystic fibrosis by children from two 'carrier' parents.

     Let R = normal allele : let r = allele for cystic fibrosis   *(7)*

Inheritance and cystic fibrosis

Genotypes of parents

male [ ] female [ ]

male gametes

female gametes

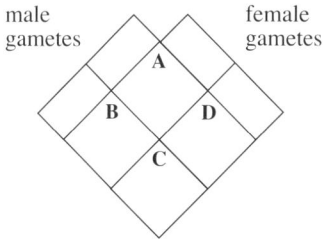

Offsping	Genotype	Phenotype
A		
B		
C		
D		

(Punnett diamond with cells labelled A, B, C, D)

b Two 'carrier' parents have two children, neither of whom show any symptoms of cystic fibrosis. What is the chance that a third child will have cystic fibrosis? *(2)*

It is possible to use a gene probe to detect the cystic fibrosis allele – the probe is able to bind onto this allele in a sample of a person's DNA. The DNA is collected from blood.

c Which type of blood cell supplies the DNA for the test? Explain your answer. *(2)*

4 Haemophilia is a sex-linked inherited characteristic. The allele (n) for haemophilia is recessive to the allele (N) for normal blood-clotting.
The gene responsible for blood-clotting is carried only on the X chromosome.

The phenotype of an organism is the appearance or characteristic that results from the inheritance of a particular combination of alleles.

a Describe the phenotypes of individuals with the following alleles *(4)*

Sex-linkage

A X Y n	Sex
	Blood clotting
B X X n N	Sex
	Blood clotting

b Use genetic symbols to explain how two non-haemophiliac parents could have a haemophiliac son. *(4)*

c Explain why haemophiliac females are less common than haemophiliac males, *(1)*

d Explain why haemophilia is especially dangerous for girls. *(1)*

1 The diagram shows a short sequence of bases in DNA.

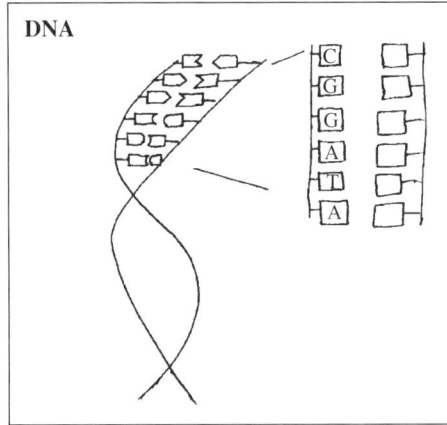

a Write out the sequence of bases on the other strand of the DNA molecule. *(2)*
b A sequence of three bases carries a code for another type of biological molecule.
   What is the name of this type of molecule? *(1)*
c The type of molecule named in part **b** is built up into larger molecules, and
   these molecules determine the characteristics of organisms.
   i   What is the general name given to these larger molecules? *(1)*
   ii Name the molecule, present in red blood cells, which gives the
       characteristic 'oxygen transport' *(1)*

2 Chromosomes contain DNA. Each individual, with very few exceptions, has different
   DNA. The DNA can be broken up, and the pieces used to produce a 'genetic fingerprint'.
   The diagram shows the genetic fingerprints of blood found at a murder scene and from
   blood samples provided by five suspects.

Fill in the missing words in the
following sentences.

a The chromosomes are found inside the
   ....of the cell. *(1)*
b Genetic fingerprints must be made from
   the ....blood cells of a suspect. *(1)*
c The murderer was most likely to be
   suspect .... *(1)*
d Genetic fingerprints can only be
   identical if they come from .... *(1)*

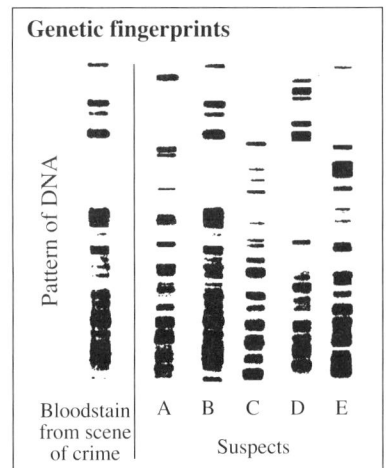

Genetic fingerprints

Pattern of DNA

Bloodstain from scene of crime | A B C D E

Suspects

Genetic fingerprinting can also be useful in conservation of endangered species. Scientists can examine the DNA fingerprint from a single hair of any animal.

    e Suggest how this could be used to prevent dangerous inbreeding between rare animals kept in zoos. *(2)*

3 Scientists have found that they can use small rings of DNA called plasmids to transfer genes into bacterial cells. The bacterial cells can then manufacture the protein coded for by the gene. This process of genetic engineering can be very useful to humans, if the protein is a valuable one. The process is outlined in the diagram below.

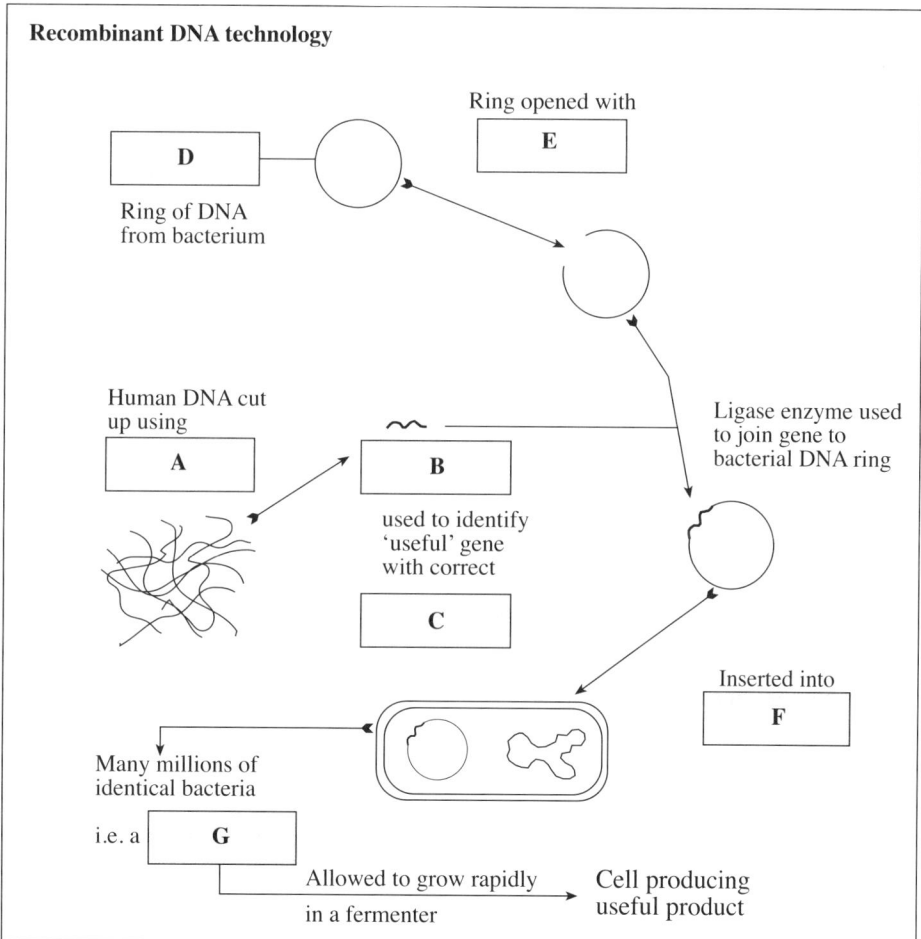

Recombinant DNA technology

Ring opened with **E**

D

Ring of DNA from bacterium

Human DNA cut up using **A**

B

used to identify 'useful' gene with correct

C

Ligase enzyme used to join gene to bacterial DNA ring

Inserted into **F**

Many millions of identical bacteria

i.e. a **G**

Allowed to grow rapidly in a fermenter

Cell producing useful product

    a Match terms from this list with the spaces left on the diagram. *(7)*

plasmid, restriction enzyme, gene probe, sequence of bases, clone, protein, bacterial cell

    b One useful protein made in this way can be used to treat diabetes. Name this protein. *(1)*

    c One possible product made by this process is *factor 8* – this protein is used to control ………… in people with the condition called ………………. *(2)*

    d Explain why some people think that genetic engineering could be dangerous. *(3)*

6 - MICROBES IN HEALTH AND DISEASE

MICROBES AND DISEASE

1   A bacterium, single-celled fungus, virus and protoctistan are examples of microorganisms.
    Arrange these organisms:

   a   in descending order of size i.e. the largest first.   *(2)*
   b   in ascending order of complexity of structure i.e the simplest first.   *(2)*
   c   For each of these microorganisms name one disease in Humans.   *(2)*

2   The diagram below shows some bacteria.

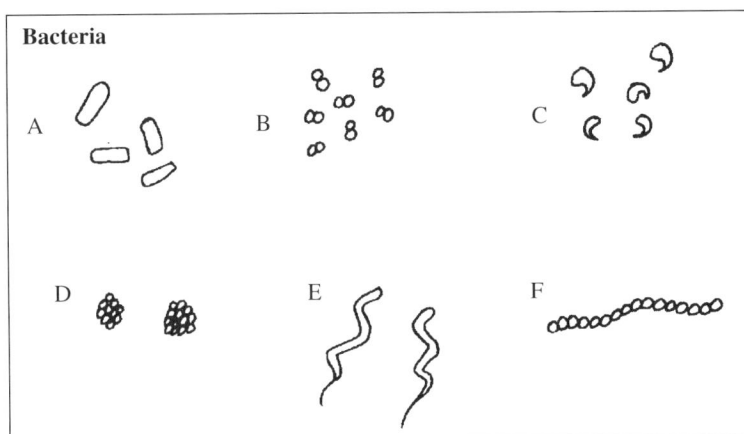

   a   Use this key to identify each bacterium.   *(6)*

1	Bacteria rod-shaped	*Bacillus*
	Bacteria not rod-shaped	Go to 2
2	Bacteria spherical in shape	Go to 3
	Bacteria not spherical in shape	Go to 5
3	Bacteria grouped in pairs	*Diplococcus*
	Bacteria not grouped in pairs	Go to 4
4	Bacteria arranged in chains	*Streptococcus*
	Bacteria arranged in clusters	*Staphylococcus*
5	Bacteria spiral shaped	*Treponema*
	Bacteria comma shaped	*Vibrio*

Treponema pallidum is responsible for a disease in Humans – this is a sexually-transmitted disease called syphilis.

   b   What steps can be taken to reduce the chances of transmitting this bacterium
        from one person to another?   *(2)*

c Bacteria can be killed outside the body by use of an antiseptic. The following investigation was carried out to study the antiseptic effects of a number of household cleansers.

2 cm³ of a bacterial culture was spread over the surface of nutrient agar in a sterile petri dish. Three wells of equal size were cut, using a cork borer sterilised by heat. The wells were then filled with 2cm³ of different cleansers. The petri dish was incubated at 30°C for 48 hours, and then examined.
The results are shown in the diagram below:

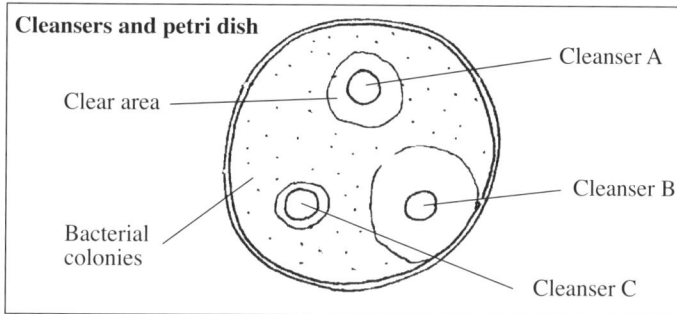

Cleansers and petri dish

i Why was it important that equal volumes of the cleansers were used? *(1)*
ii Describe and explain the results shown in the diagram *(2)*
iii Suggest a suitable control which would improve the validity of the results *(1)*
iv What is the difference between an antiseptic and an antibiotic? *(1)*

3 The diagram shows a virus, a bacterium and a fungus – they are not drawn to scale.

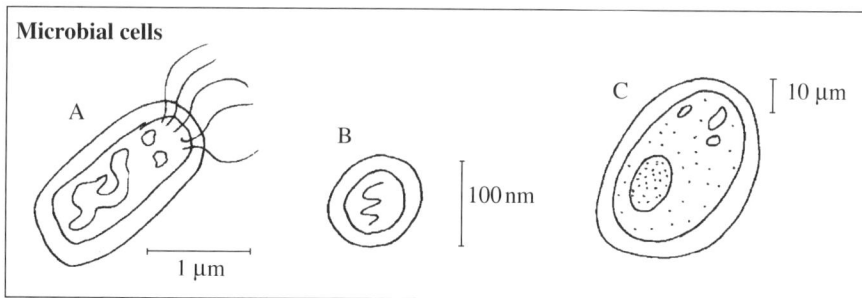

Microbial cells

a Which is the bacterium?
Give two reasons, shown in the diagram, for your answer. *(3)*
b Write down three characteristics of fungi. *(3)*
c 1 mm = 1000 μm ; 1 μm = 1000 nm.
Use this information to calculate a scale of magnification for the drawing of the virus. Show your working. *(2)*
d Viruses cannot survive and reproduce outside another living cell.
Describe one simple test for a characteristic of living organisms which would allow you to distinguish viruses from other microorganisms.
State the reagents you would use, the results you might expect, and any control experiment that you might use. *(4)*

1 Read the following passage, and then answer the questions that follow.

FLEMING, FLOREY AND CHAIN : PENICILLIN WAS THE FIRST AVAILABLE ANTIBIOTIC

The British bacteriologist Alexander Fleming was working on cultures of bacteria grown on agar plates. In 1928 he noticed that some of his plates were contaminated with mould - this was not an uncommon occurrence - but, more importantly, he noticed that the bacteria could not grow close to the mould. Fleming identified the mould as Penicillium notatum and suggested that it produced a substance which killed the bacteria. He isolated a small quantity of the substance, and called it penicillin. Fleming believed that penicillin might be useful in fighting bacterial infections, but was not able to overcome the difficulties of isolating it in large enough quantities for use in medicine.

Two chemists, Howard Florey and Ernst Chain, developed techniques for growing large quantities of the mould and for isolating penicillin from it. They began work in 1938, after reading of Fleming's observations, and soon found that the demands of the Second World War made it difficult to obtain laboratory equipment and supplies. They carried out many of their experiments in milk bottles, jamjars and even bedpans borrowed from the nearby hospital! They found that *Penicillium chrysogeneum* was a better strain than P.notatum for producing penicillin, and manufactured enough of the drug to carry out the first clinical trials. The first person to be successfully treated with penicillin, in 1940, was a policeman who had a bad wound infection and was close to death. Penicillin cleared the infection, but unfortunately there wasn't enough available for continued treatment and many of the early patients died after showing signs of recovery.

The urgent need to treat wounded soldiers meant that the production of penicillin had to be stepped up very quickly. The work moved to the United States of America where large fermenters were set up using a waste product of the starch industry as a nutrient solution for the growth of the mould. By 1944, doctors had enough penicillin to treat all the British and American casualties of the Normandy landings. The knowledge of this 'wonder drug' was a great morale-booster for the Allied troops.

By the 1950's penicillin was available for widespread use throughout the general population. It is interesting to note that the most antibiotic-resistant bacterium - MRSA - is a strain of *Staphylococcus aureus*, the bacterium on which Alexander Fleming was working when he made his initial observations!

a Penicillin is an antibiotic - what is meant by the term 'antibiotic'? *(1)*
b Why do you think Fleming called his antibiotic 'penicillin'? *(1)*
c What did Florey and Chain do to improve the availability of penicillin? *(2)*
d Penicillin production was transferred to the USA during the Second World War. What food source was used in the large-scale fermenters for penicillin production? *(1)*

The graph over the page shows the amounts of *Penicillium* fungus and penicillin in a fermenter over a 10-day period.

e What is the best time to collect the penicillin? Explain your answer. *(2)*

f Antibiotic-resistant strains of bacteria are very dangerous in present-day hospitals. Use a diagram to explain how mutation and selection can produce a large population of antibiotic-resistant bacteria. *(3)*

Penicillin production

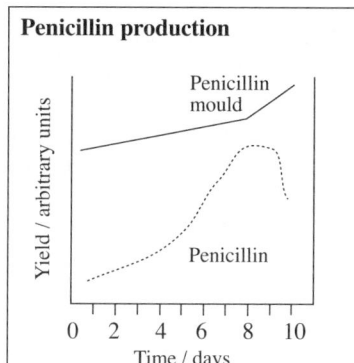

2 Fungi may grow on Human skin, making it itch and become inflamed. Some medical students were interested in how to prevent skin becoming infected with fungi. They were able to obtain samples of living skin, and grow them on a special base which supplies nutrients but keeps the skin surface dry. The skin could be moistened by a gentle spray of water. They used four samples of skin from the same donor, and treated them as shown in the Table below.

Skin section	Temperature/°C	Condition
1	20	Moist
2	20	Dry
3	30	Moist
4	30	dry

The skin sections were allowed to grow as shown in this diagram.

The sections were examined after 10 days. The results are shown below:

Skin growth chamber

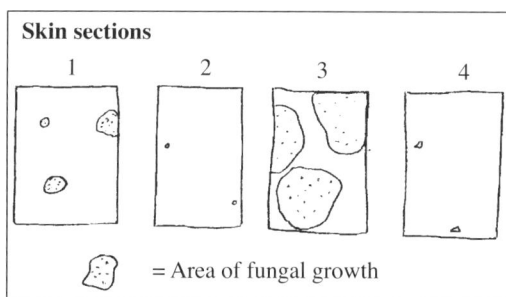

Skin sections

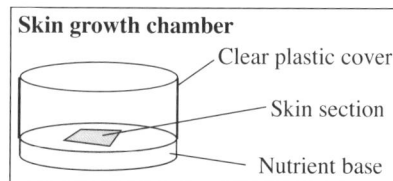

= Area of fungal growth

a Why is it important that the four skin sections came from the same donor? *(1)*

b i The students identified two conditions that reduce the growth of fungi on the skin surface. What are these conditions? *(2)*

ii Only one of these conditions can be applied to a living Human. Which one would not be a sensible method of limiting fungi on living Human skin? Explain your answer. *(2)*

c Name one fungal disease of human skin *(1)*

d Why does antibiotic cream have no effect on fungal diseases? *(1)*

53

1   The diagram shows the sequence of operations in the activated sludge process for water
    treatment. Match the labels with the stages in the process.   *(10)*

    A sewage input   B sludge   C methane
    D gas pumps   E activated sludge   F treated water into river
    G screen   H digester   I product sold as fertiliser

Sewage treatment

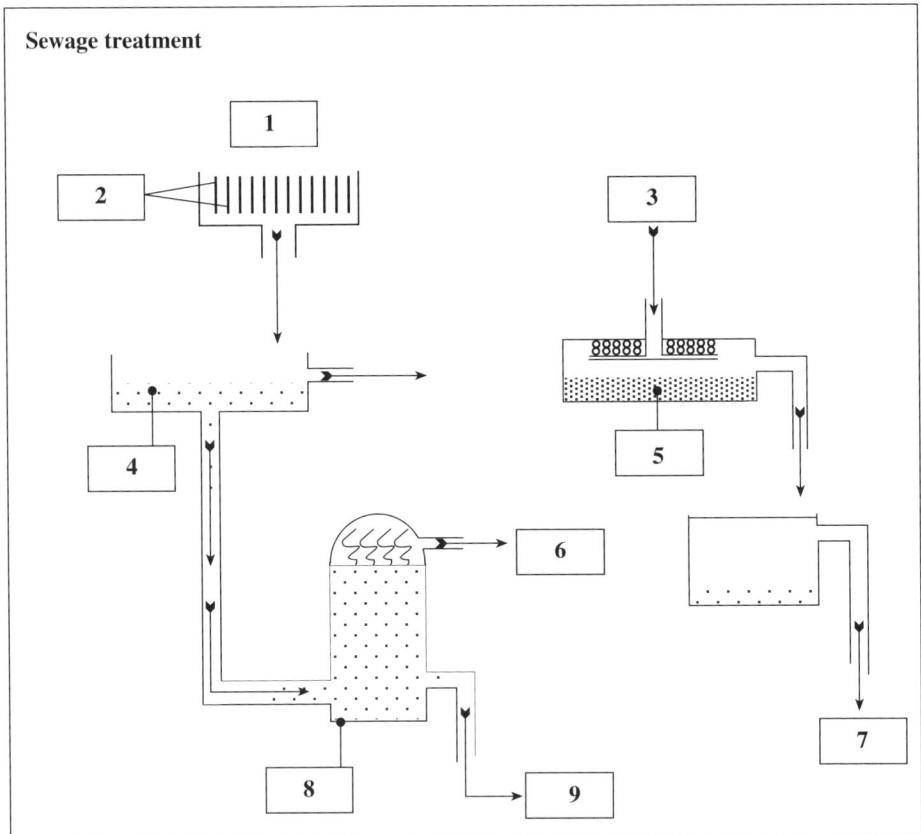

2   Cheese is made using milk. The milk can be supplied by many different animals.
    The table shows the composition of three different types of milk.

Source of milk	Mass of substance (g per 100g milk)				
	Carbohydrate	Fat	Protein	Minerals	Water
Sheep	5.0	9.5	4.5	1.0	80.0
Goat	5.1	6.0	3.5	0.7	84.7
Cow	5.1	3.5	3.0	0.8	87.6

   a   To make soft cheese the whey (a liquid containing 50% of the water and all of the
       carbohydrate) is removed.
       100g of cows' milk makes 51.1g of soft cheese.
       How much soft cheese is made from 100g of goats' milk? Show your working.   *(2)*

b Each gram of carbohydrate can be respired to 18 kJ of energy.
What is the energy content of the whey separated from 100g of sheeps' milk?
Show your working. *(2)*

c The flow chart shows a scheme for the industrial production of cheese.
Match the labels to the stages of the process. *(6)*

A   bacteria break down proteins and fats   B   addition of chymosin or rennin
C   water   D   whey   E   hard cheese   F   fresh milk

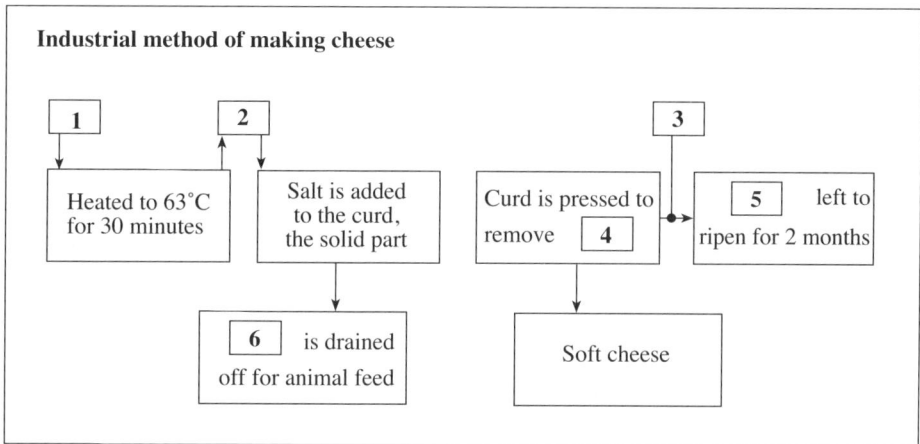

Industrial method of making cheese

| 1 | 2 | 3 |

| Heated to 63°C for 30 minutes | Salt is added to the curd, the solid part | Curd is pressed to remove 4 | 5 left to ripen for 2 months |

| 6 is drained off for animal feed | | Soft cheese |

3   The diagram shows the sequence of processes involved in the manufacture of Soy sauce.

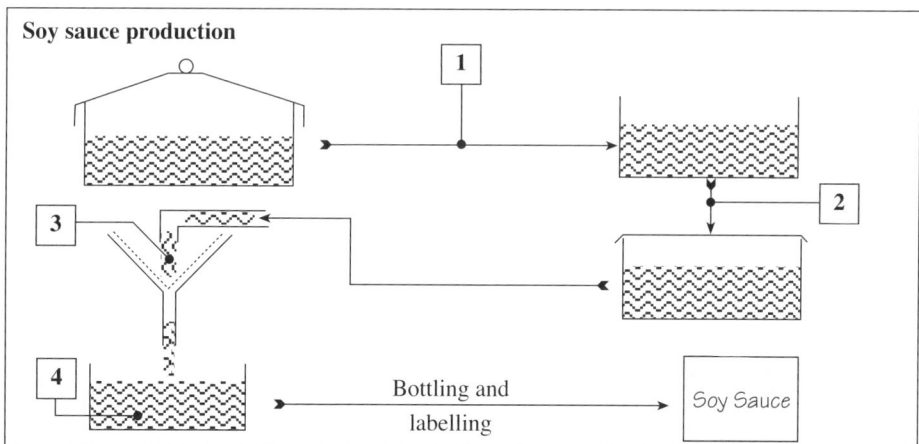

Soy sauce production

1

2

3

4

Bottling and labelling   Soy Sauce

a Name the organism involved in the anaerobic fermentation at stage 2. *(1)*
b What is the purpose of the stage labelled 3? *(1)*
c At stage 4 the product is pasteurised. Why is this important? *(2)*
d Stage 1 includes aerobic respiration of sugar.
Write a word equation for this process. *(2)*
e Suggest two pieces of nutritional information which should be included
on the label for the bottled product. *(2)*

1 The diagram shows the production of yoghurt from milk.
   a Match terms from this list to the stages in the process. *(6)*

   casein, incubation, homogenisation, cooling, lactose, pasteurisation

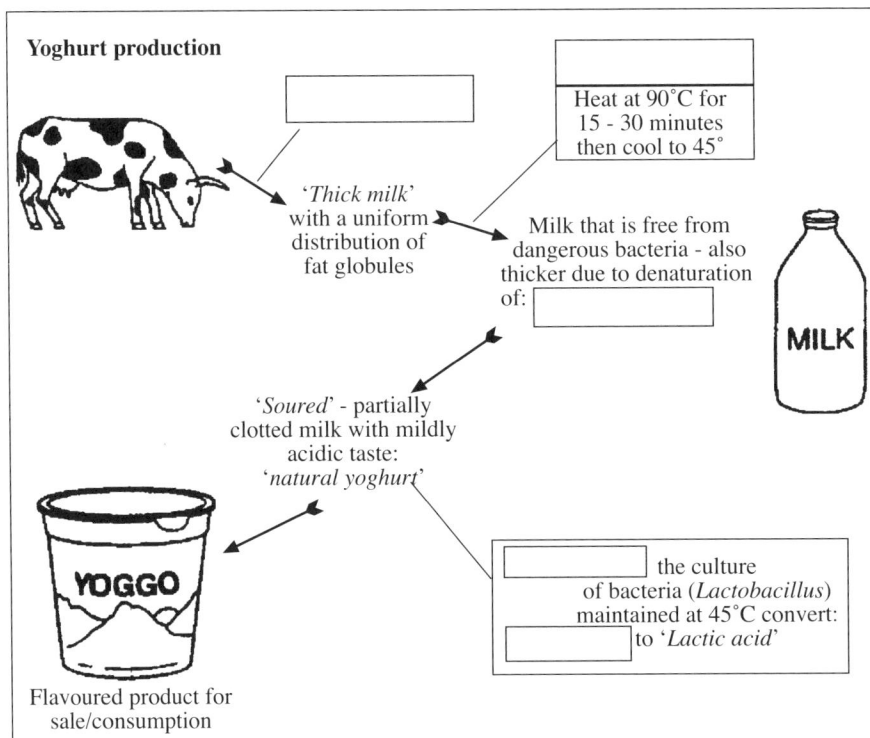

Yoghurt production

'Thick milk' with a uniform distribution of fat globules

Heat at 90°C for 15 - 30 minutes then cool to 45°

Milk that is free from dangerous bacteria - also thicker due to denaturation of:

MILK

'Soured' - partially clotted milk with mildly acidic taste: *'natural yoghurt'*

YOGGO

the culture of bacteria (*Lactobacillus*) maintained at 45°C convert: to *'Lactic acid'*

Flavoured product for sale/consumption

   b State the genus of the microbe involved in lowering the pH of the yoghurt *(1)*

   The table lists some of the contents of flavoured yoghurt.

Substance present	Fat	Protein	Calcium	Vitamins	Sugar	Others
Mass of substance (g per 100g)	2.2	1.8	Less than 1.0	Less than 1.0	9.8	85

   c State one use of the calcium in a healthy diet. *(1)*
   d Which compound will make up the greatest proportion of the 'others' category? *(1)*
   e One gram of protein can be respired to release 18 kJ of energy, one gram of carbohydrate releases 17 kJ of energy and one gram of fat yields 35 kJ of energy. What is the total energy content of a 25g serving of this fruit yoghurt? Show your working. *(3)*

2   The diagram shows the layout of one type of sewage treatment works.

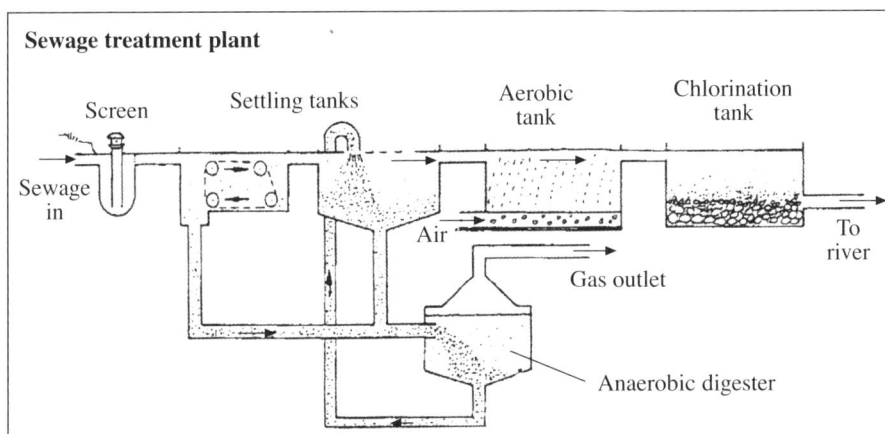

Sewage treatment plant

a   Describe the part played by aerobic bacteria in this type of sewage treatment works. *(2)*
b   Name the useful gas produced by the anaerobic digester. *(1)*
c   Why is this gas useful? *(1)*
d   This gas can also be a pollutant – explain why. *(2)*
e   Explain what might happen if the treatment failed, and sewage was allowed to enter the river. *(3)*
f   Explain the function of the chlorination tank *(1)*

3   Read the paragraphs below, and then answer the questions that follow.

Single cell protein may be used as a source of food for humans

One well-developed example of a bioreactor/fermenter is used to produce 'fungi' for consumption by Humans. This product, called mycoprotein, is an example of single-cell protein. The mycoprotein which is eaten nowadays is made from the compacted hyphae of the fungus *Fusarium graminearum*. This offers a number of advantages as a food source
·   It can be produced very quickly – the fungus doubles its mass within hours.
·   It can be produced cheaply – the fungus can use waste materials from other processes e.g. the waste carbohydrate from flour production, or cheaply-available 'foods' such as sugar beet, on which to grow.
·   It has a high protein content (40%), at least as high as beefsteak.
·   It has a much lower fat content (only 13%) but much higher fibre content than meat.
·   The mycelium of hyphae can be easily shaped and flavoured.
Fusarium is grown in continuous culture, with a 'harvest' being collected every two or three weeks. The collected fungus is separated from the culture medium, washed in steam and then frozen or dried before processing into other food products.

a   What, exactly, is mycoprotein? *(2)*
b   Give two reasons why mycoprotein is a healthy alternative to meat. Explain your answers. *(4)*
c   Mycoprotein is harvested every 15 – 20 days. Draw a flow diagram to explain what happens to the mycoprotein from the time it leaves the fermenter until it is ready for sale. *(4)*

1   It is possible to conduct simple chemical tests to investigate the chemical content of
    biological solutions. Usually these tests involve mixing reagents with the solution, and
    noting any colour change. The following results were obtained from a series of tests.

Solution	Colour after testing with reagent			
	Iodine solution	Benedict's reagent	Biuret reagent	Benedict's after acidification and neutralisation
A	Blue-black	Clear blue	Clear blue	Clear blue
B	Straw-yellow	Orange	Purple	Orange
C	Straw yellow	Clear blue	Clear blue	Orange
D	Blue-black	Clear blue	Faint purple	Clear blue
E	Straw yellow	Orange	Clear blue	Orange

    Suggest which of these solutions might be:

    a the waste water from a laundry.   (1)
    b milk   (1)
    c crushed potato   (1)
    d urine from a sufferer of sugar diabetes   (1)
    e sweetened tea   (1)

    In each case give a reason for your choice.

2   The diagram shows a cell from the pancreas of a human.
    The cell was drawn using a light microscope.

    a Identify the structures labelled A, B and C.   (3)
    b Which of these structures would not be present
       in a red blood cell?   (1)
    c Name two additional structures that you would
       see in a palisade cell from a leaf.   (2)
    d Use the scale shown alongside the cell to
       calculate how much it has been magnified.
       Show your working.   (3)

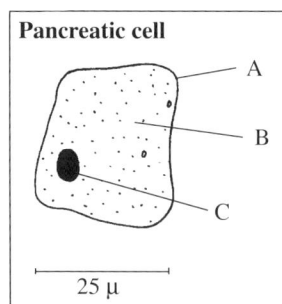

Pancreatic cell

25 µ

3   An experiment was set up to try to measure the concentration of the cytoplasm inside
    potato cells. A cork borer was used to produce identical cylinders of potato tissue.
    Twenty one of these cylinders were blotted dry, weighed, and then three were placed into
    each of seven boiling tubes labelled A – G. The boiling tubes contained a series of sugar
    solutions, ranging from 0.0 to 0.6 molar.

Two hours later the cylinders were removed from the tubes, blotted dry and reweighed. The results are shown in the Table below:

Tube	A	B	C	D	E	F	G
Concentration of sugar solution/molar	0.0	0.1	0.2	0.3	0.4	0.5	0.6
Percentage change in mass of potato cylinders	+10	+6	+2	-3	-7	-10	-12

a Plot a graph of percentage change in mass against concentration of sucrose solution. *(4)*

b Use your graph to state the concentration of sucrose solution that will give no change in mass of the potato tissue. *(2)*

c Use your biological knowledge to explain how this value allows you to work out the concentration of the cytoplasm in the potato cells. *(2)*

d Explain why three potato cylinders were placed into each of the solutions. *(2)*

e Explain why the potato cylinders are blotted dry before they are weighed. *(2)*

f Three more potato cylinders were placed into a 1 molar solution of sucrose. The potato cylinders weighed a total of 10 g. Predict the mass of this tissue after two hours in this solution. *(2)*

4 The diagram shows the energy flow in a food chain in a pond over a period of one year. The figures show the units of light energy which fall on the pond and the units of energy passed along the food chain to each of four trophic levels, and the units of energy released in respiration and passing to decomposers.

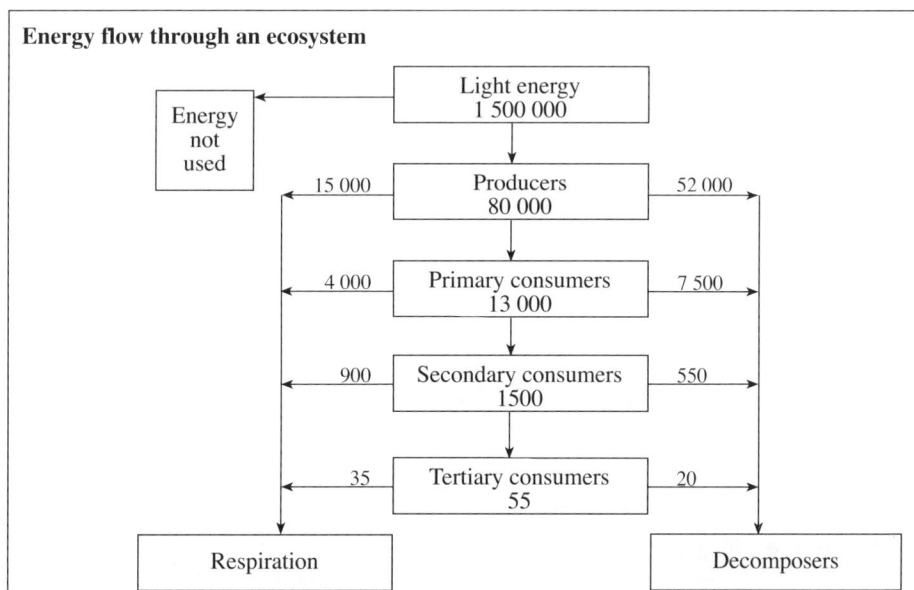

Energy flow through an ecosystem

Energy not used	Light energy 1 500 000
15 000	Producers 80 000 — 52 000
4 000	Primary consumers 13 000 — 7 500
900	Secondary consumers 1500 — 550
35	Tertiary consumers 55 — 20
Respiration	Decomposers

a What is the source of energy for the pond? *(1)*

b How many units of energy were not used by the producers to form their body mass? *(2)*

c Calculate the percentage of light energy converted into body mass by the producers. Show your working. *(2)*

d What happened to the large amount of energy that was not used by the producers? *(2)*

e How many units of energy passed to the decomposers in the pond during the year? *(2)*

f Bacteria form one group of decomposers.
Name another group of decomposers that are not plants or animals. *(2)*

g The activities of the living organisms release a gas that turns the pondwater slightly acid. What is this gas, and what is the name of the process that releases it? *(2)*

5 The diagram shows part of the human circulation.

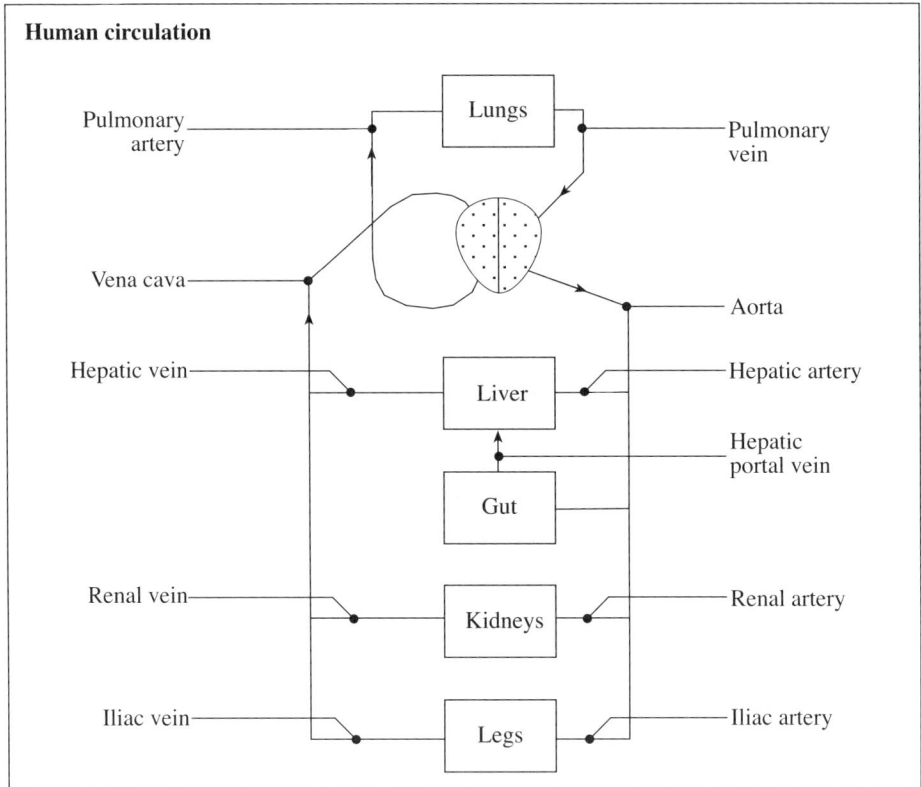

Human circulation

a Name the blood vessels and chambers of the heart through which:

   i a molecule of amino acid absorbed by the gut passes on its way to build up muscle in the heart. *(3)*

   ii a red blood cell passes as it delivers oxygen from the lungs to the liver and returns to be reoxygenated. *(3)*

A poster in a doctor's surgery had the headline:

A HEALTHY LIFESTYLE MEANS A HEALTHY HEART

b Suggest two features of a person's lifestyle that would give them a good chance of having a healthy heart. *(2)*

c Suggest two different features of one's lifestyle that might lead to heart disease. *(2)*

6 In labradors, black fur is dominant to golden fur. Copy and complete the genetic diagram to show how a heterozygous black male labrador and a golden female labrador can produce a litter containing some golden offspring.

Let B = allele for black fur,
let b = allele for golden fur   *(5)*

Labrador inheritance

Parental phenotypes		Black ♂ × Golden ♀	
Parental genotypes		☐ × bb	
Gametes		○ b / ○ b	
Offspring genotypes		☐ : bb	
Offspring phenotypes		Black : Golden	
Offspring ratio		☐ : ☐	

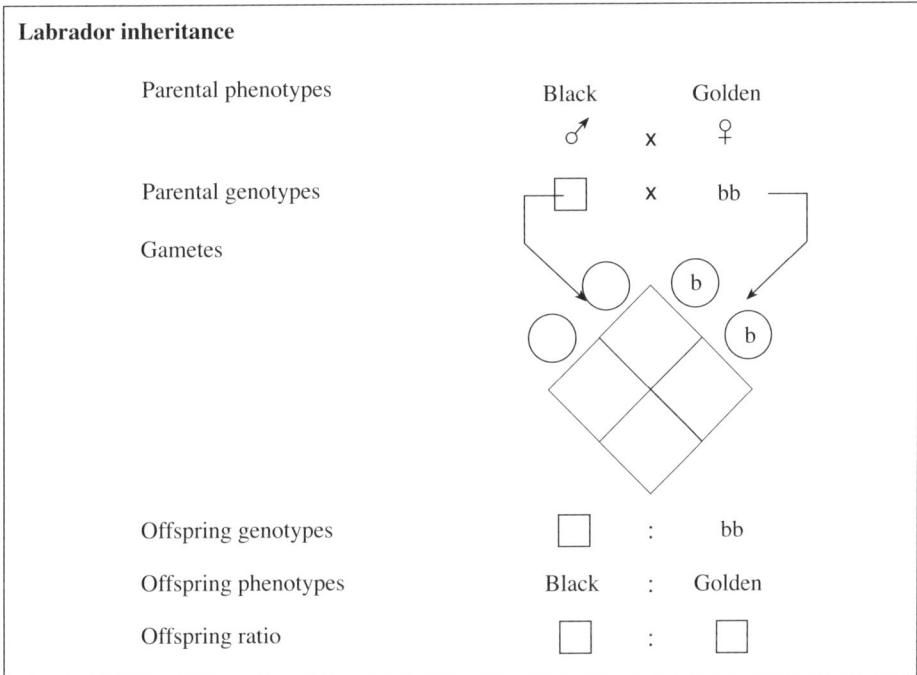

7 The diagram shows a cross-section of part of a leaf. The section has been viewed through a microscope.

a Which of the labelled structures:
  i brings water to the leaf
  ii takes sugar away from the leaf
  iii allows carbon dioxide to enter the leaf?   *(3)*

Leaf section

Waxy cuticle, Epidermal cells, One chloroplast, Palisade cells, Xylem, Spongy cells, Phloem, Stoma, Guard cells, Epidermal cells

b Sugars are produced in some of the leaf cells, and then may be transported to other parts of the plant.
  i Write out a word equation for the process that produces the sugars.   *(2)*
  ii Suggest two uses for the sugar that is transported to other parts of the plant.   *(2)*

c **i** What is the substance in the chloroplasts that absorbs light?
  ii Name the mineral ion needed to make this substance.   *(2)*

d The leaves of grasses living on sand dunes are often rolled up. Why is this?   *(1)*

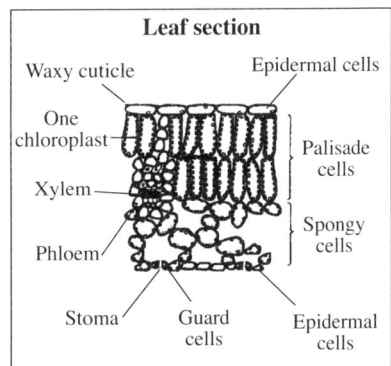

8 Some students wanted to investigate the frequency of a certain 'weed' growing on the school lawn. They used a 1 m² quadrat, and then marked on an outline of the quadrat the position of each of individual weed. Six of the quadrats are drawn out in the diagram:

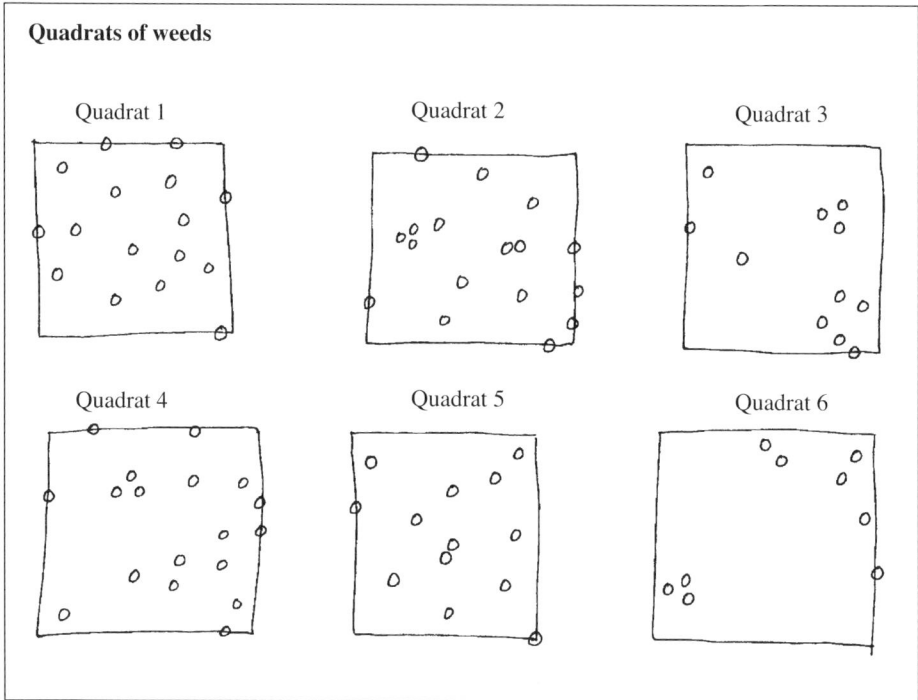

Quadrats of weeds

Quadrat 1　　Quadrat 2　　Quadrat 3

Quadrat 4　　Quadrat 5　　Quadrat 6

a Count the number of weed plants in each quadrat.
Copy the table below, and record your results in it.
Count plants which tough the upper and left hand sides of the square as 'in', but those that touch the lower and right hand sides of the square as 'out'. *(2)*

Quadrat number	1	2	3	4	5	6
Number of weed plants						

b Work out the average number of plants per m² for the six squares.
Show your working. *(2)*

c There were four parts to the lawn: part 1 was 40 m², part 2 was 55 m², part 3 was 145 m², and part 4 was 410 m².
How many weed plants would you expect in the whole lawn? Show your working. *(2)*

d Suggest two natural environmental factors that might affect how many weed plants there were on the lawn. *(2)*

e Suggest two artificial (human) factors that might affect how many weed plants there were on the lawn. *(2)*

9 The sex of most animals is determined by their sex cells (gametes). It is these cells which combine to form a new organism. The diagram shows a male gamete from a human.

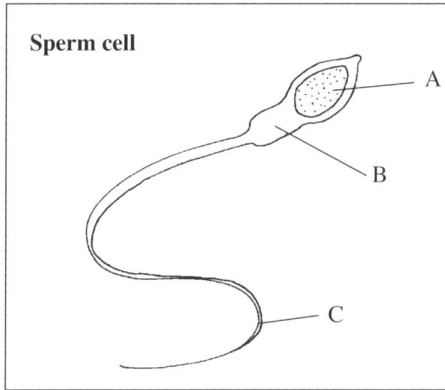

a Name the type of cell division which produces gametes.   (1)
b State the major difference between a gamete and a normal cell.   (1)
c The part labelled A carries the instructions that will help to form the new organism.
   The instructions are carried as a chemical code.
   Name the chemical that carries these instructions.   (1)
d When a male and female gamete join together at fertilisation a zygote is formed.
   The zygote divides many times to become an embryo, and eventually a baby organism.
   During this division the 'information chemical' is copied accurately.
   The diagram shows a section of this chemical during this copying.
   Draw a completed version of the diagram by adding the correct code letters.   (2)

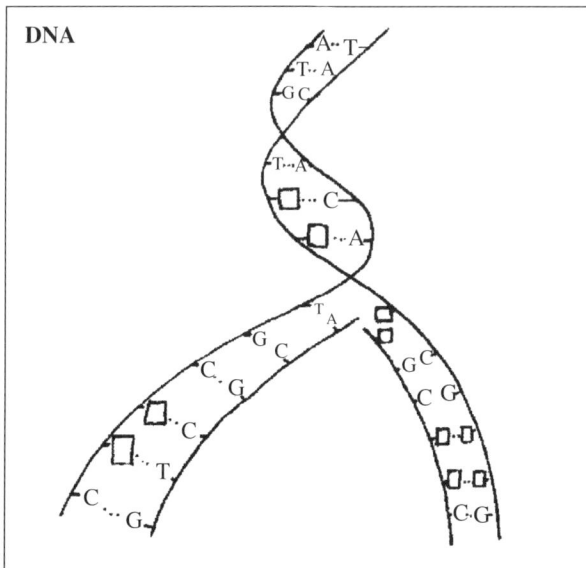

e Sometimes the copying process goes wrong, and faulty information is made.
   What is the name given to the process causing 'faulty' copying?   (1)
f Name one environmental factor that might increase the risk of this faulty copying.   (1)
g Name one human disease caused by a fault of this type.   (1)

1 Simple chemical tests on foods can show which type of nutrients they contain.

A group of students was given samples of four different foods to test – the samples were prepared by dissolving powdered food in distilled water. The four foods were identified as A, B, C and D. They were also given a sample of distilled water.

They carried out three tests on the five samples. Test 1 was for glucose, Test 2 was for protein and Test 3 was for starch. The results of the tests are shown in the table.

Food test	1: glucose	2: protein	3: starch
Sample A	Blue	Purple	Brown
Sample B	Orange	Blue	Brown
Sample C	Blue	Blue	Black
Sample D	Orange	Purple	Brown
Distilled water	Blue	Blue	Brown

a Which colour indicates the presence of starch?   *(1)*
b What is the name of the solution which gives a purple colour if protein is present? *(1)*
c Which one of the samples contained protein and glucose but no starch?   *(1)*
d Why were the tests also carried out on distilled water?   *(1)*
e This series of tests does not detect the presence of fat.
   Describe a test for fat, including a positive result for the test.   *(3)*
f Explain one danger to health of eating too many foods which contain large
   amounts of fat.   *(1)*

2 The diagram shows the human breathing system.

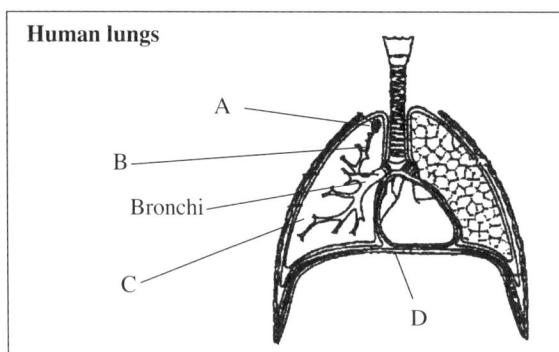

a Match the labelling letters on the diagram with names from the following list.   *(4)*

   air sac, diaphragm, heart, larynx, trachea, lung, bronchiole

b Complete the paragraphs on the next page, using terms from this list.
   You may use each term once, more than once, or not at all.   *(10)*

   upwards, diaphragm, volume, increases, decreases, trachea,
   downwards, tar, nicotine, lungs, cancer

When we breathe in the ribs move .... and outwards because the intercostal muscles contract. At the same time the .... contracts and moves .... As a result the .... of the lungs .... and the air pressure inside them .... If the mouth and the nose are open, air can rush down the .... Into the ....

The efficiency of the lungs can be reduced by smoking. For example, the tar in cigarette smoke can make cells divide out of control, causing ....
Another component of the tobacco smoke, ..., causes the heart to beat faster and the blood pressure to rise.

3 The diagram shows the chemical changes which occur during the process of respiration.

a Copy the diagram and add the missing labels. *(3)*

Humming birds are small birds which feed by sipping nectar from flowers. The graph below shows the relationship between body mass and oxygen consumption for various species of humming bird.

Cell respiration

Glucose

Water

Work

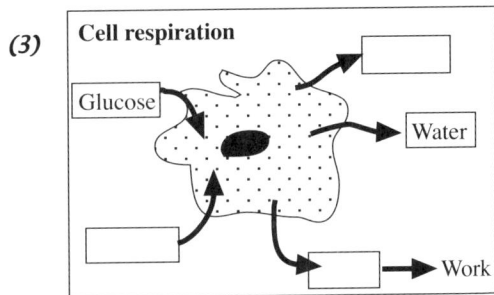

Oxygen consumption for humming birds

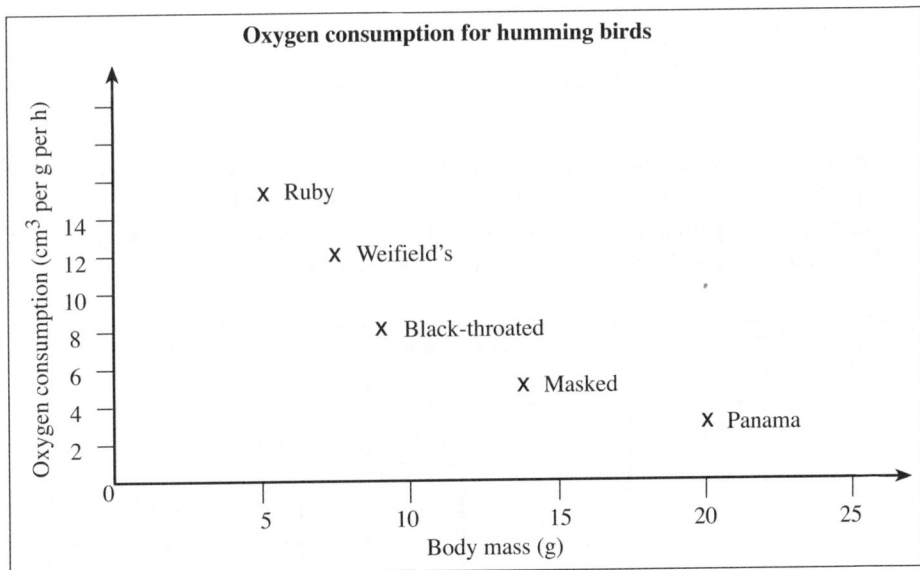

b Which species of humming bird uses 5 cm³ of oxygen per gram per hour? *(1)*
c How much greater is the oxygen consumption of the Weifeld's Humming bird than that of the Panama Humming bird?
   Give your answer as a percentage, and show your working. *(3)*
d Suggest a reason for the difference noted in part **c**. *(2)*
e A hummingbird may drink 90% of its own body mass in nectar every day. Which species would drink the greatest amount of nectar?
   How much would it drink? Show your working. *(3)*

4 The diagram shows the food web for an ecosystem based on a birch tree.

a Write out one complete food chain involving five organisms. *(2)*

b Food chains are rarely as long as the one you have drawn. Why not? *(2)*

c What is the producer in this food web? *(1)*

d What can the producer do that no other organism in the food web is capable of? *(1)*

e A gamekeeper decided to trap and kill the hawks and foxes in the woodland.
Explain two effects that this might have on other organisms in the food web. *(2)*

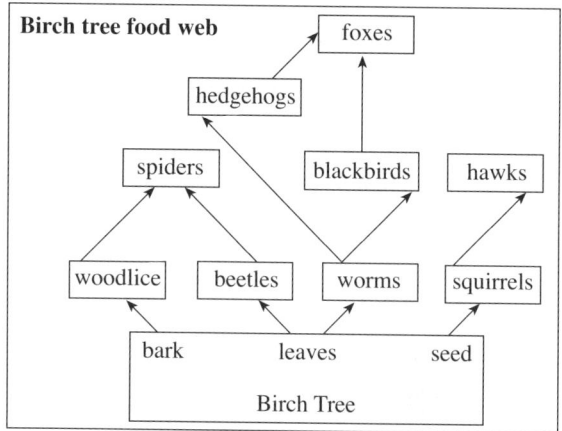

Birch tree food web

foxes

hedgehogs

spiders   blackbirds   hawks

woodlice   beetles   worms   squirrels

bark   leaves   seed

Birch Tree

5 The fur of a mouse is normally straight, but there is a mutation which causes 'curly' fur. The diagram below shows mice with these characteristics.

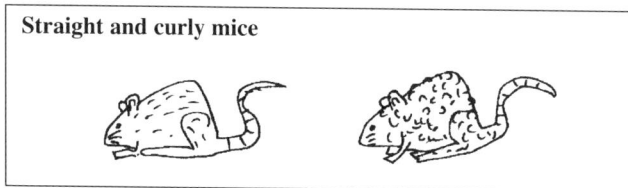

Straight and curly mice

Crosses between pure-breeding (homozygous) straight-haired mice and pure-breeding curly-haired mice produced F_1 offspring which all had straight fur.
The F_1 offspring from many crosses were allowed to mate to produce many F_2 offspring. The results of these F_1 crosses are shown in the table below.

Group	Male mice		Female mice	
	Straight fur	Curly fur	Straight fur	Curly fur
1	7	0	6	1
2	4	2	5	1
3	6	3	6	2
4	4	1	5	2
5	3	2	5	3
6	5	1	4	2
7	3	1	3	0
8	6	2	4	1
9	5	2	5	2
10	4	1	5	1
Total	47	15	48	15

a This variation in coat form is caused by two different forms of the same gene. What is the name given to different forms of the same gene? *(1)*

b Which of these two forms, straight or curly, is dominant? *(1)*

c Use a genetic diagram to explain the ratio between the two different forms, shown by the 'total' figures in the table. *(4)*

d Explain why the actual ratio is not exactly the one you would predict. *(2)*

6 The diagram shows how human *factor 8* can be made by genetic engineering.

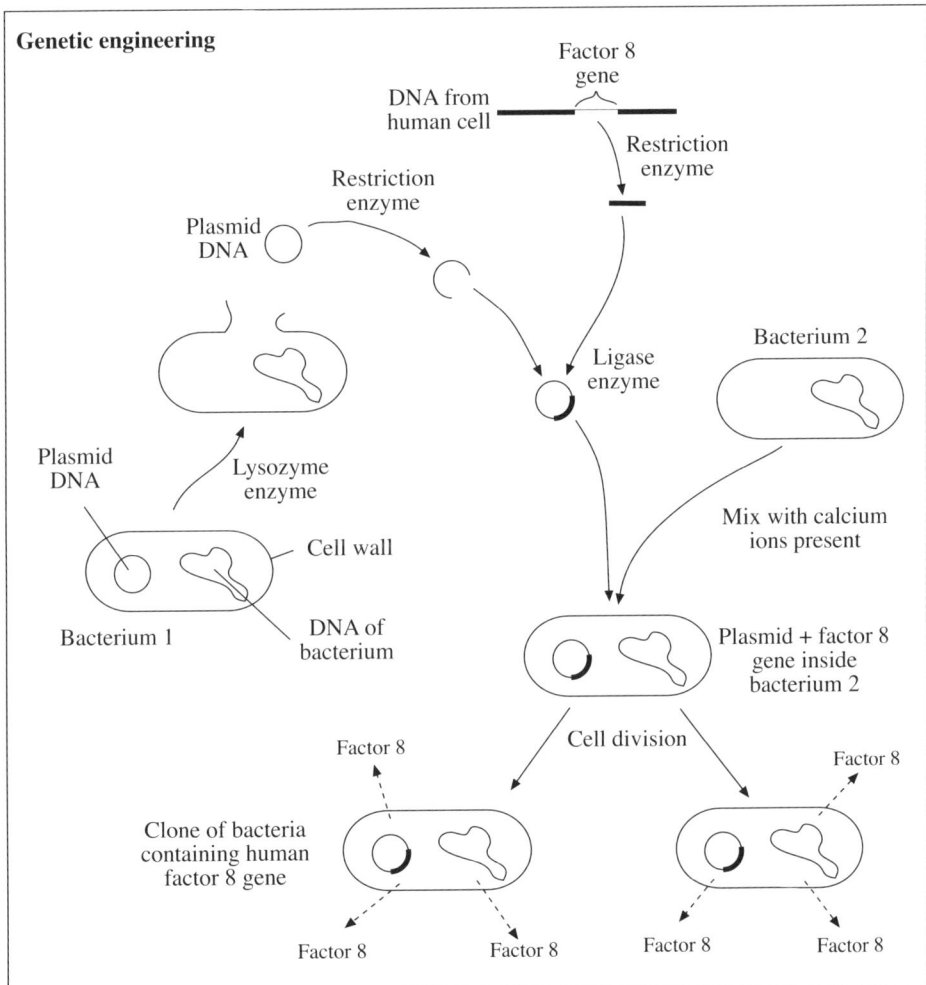

Genetic engineering

a Using only the information from the diagram describe how the gene for *factor 8* is put into a bacterium. *(7)*

b Why is *factor 8* valuable? *(1)*

c Name one other human protein that can be made by genetic engineering, and state why it is so useful. *(2)*

d A bacterium which has been altered in this way is a *genetically-modified organism* (GMO). Why are some people against the use of GMOs? *(2)*

7 The diagram shows a section through a single kidney.

Single kidney

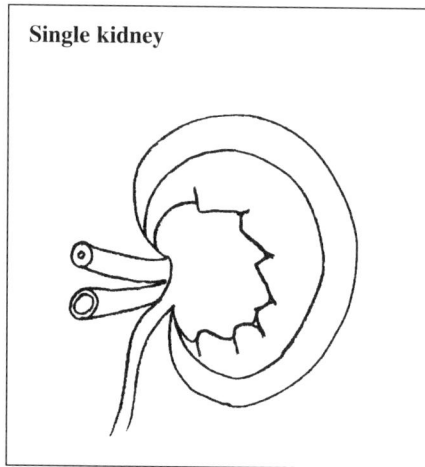

a Copy this outline.

b On the outline label the medulla, renal artery, renal vein, ureter, cortex (5)

c Label with an X the region of the kidney where filtration of the blood occurs (1)

d Label with a Y a structure in which peristalsis occurs. (1)

e Label with a Z the region which would be larger in a gerbil but smaller in a beaver. (1)

8 The table below shows the human population of the world from the year 1700 to 2000.

Year	Population (millions)
1700	700
1750	800
1800	900
1850	1100
1900	2200
1950	3600
2000	6000

a Plot this information in the form of a line graph. (4)

b Suggest two reasons for the rapid increase in population between 1850 and 2000. (2)

c If the world population continues to increase, what will be the likely effect on:

  i deforestation (2)

  ii farming (2)

1 The diagram shows a pathway of a reflex action.

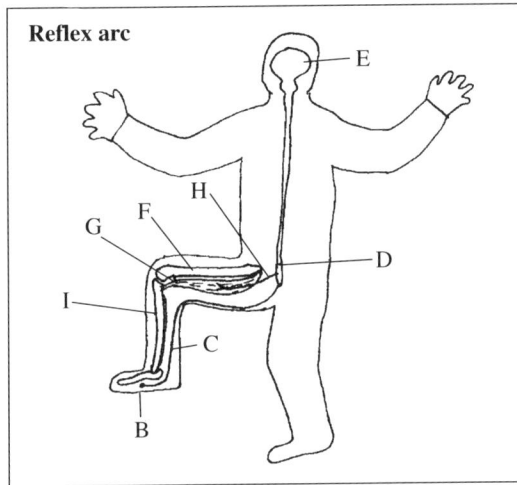

a Match the letters with the following descriptions: *(5)*

    1   an effector
    2   a receptor
    3   an integrator
    4   a sensory neurone
    5   a motor neurone

b What is meant by the term stimulus?   *(1)*
c Suggest a stimulus that could start this reflex action.   *(1)*
d The reflex action would bring about a response.
    What is the value of the response in this example?   *(1)*
e What is a conditioned reflex? Give one example of this kind of behaviour. *(2)*

2 The diagram shows part of a food web on a seashore.

a Note the following feeding relationships.
    A Mussels feed on plankton, but are
       eaten by dogwhelks and by gulls
    B Crabs eat periwinkles and seaweed,
       but are eaten by gulls
    C Gulls also eat dogwhelks
    Copy out the food web, and complete it
    using the information above.   *(5)*
b i Which process must the seaweed
    and plankton carry out to support
    this food web?   *(1)*
ii Write out a word equation for
    this process.   *(2)*

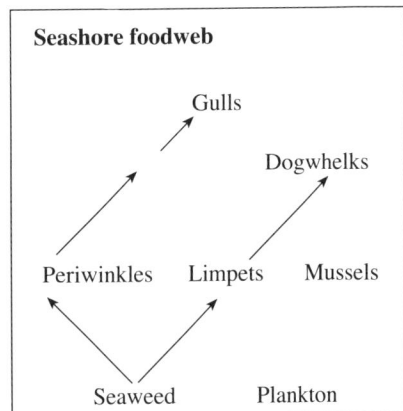

Seashore foodweb

69

c This seashore is near a factory which makes detergents.
Sometimes the detergents get into the sea, and cause the death of limpets.
How would the death of the limpets affect the population of dogwhelks?
Explain your answer. *(2)*

3 a A biology student working in a museum mixed up a series of specimens.
The specimens are named in this list:

*amphibian, earthworm, bacterium, bird, mammal, fish, reptile, fungus,
moss, fern, protoctistan, virus, flowering plant, insect, parasite*

Choose organisms from this list to match the following descriptions: *(7)*
i Body covered with fur, has mammary glands
ii Cells with cell wall but no chlorophyll. Reproduce by spores
iii Body covered with dry scales
iv Body has three regions – head, thorax and abdomen
v Single cell, without definite nucleus
vi Can only reproduce within another living cell; few genes inside protein coat
vii Feathers, beak, maintains constant body temperature

b All living organisms display certain characteristics.
Complete the following sentences about these characteristics.
i Releasing energy in cells is called ………………………… *(1)*
ii The removal of the waste products of the chemical processes
in the body is called ……………………… *(1)*
iii The ability to respond to changes in the environment is called …………… *(1)*

4 The ability to taste the chemical PTC (which is very bitter) is an example of discontinuous variation. It results from the presence of a dominant allele, T, in the genotype.

a What is meant by discontinuous variation? *(1)*
b Give another example of discontinuous variation in Humans *(1)*
c Explain what is meant by the term genotype. *(1)*

The diagram shows a family history of 'tasting' over three generations.

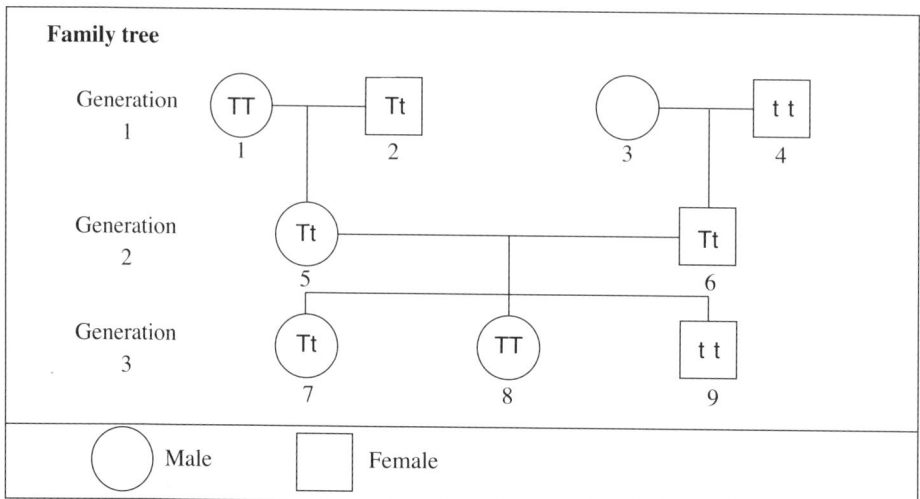

Family tree

Generation 1	TT (1) — Tt (2)			(3) — t t (4)	
Generation 2		Tt (5) —		Tt (6)	
Generation 3		Tt (7)	TT (8)	t t (9)	

○ Male   ☐ Female

d Which individual in generation three is a heterozygote? *(1)*

e What are the possible genotypes of individual 3? *(2)*

f individual 7 marries a woman with the same genotype.

Copy and complete the Punnett Square to show the possible genotypes of their children *(3)*

g What is the probability that their second child will be able to taste PTC? *(1)*

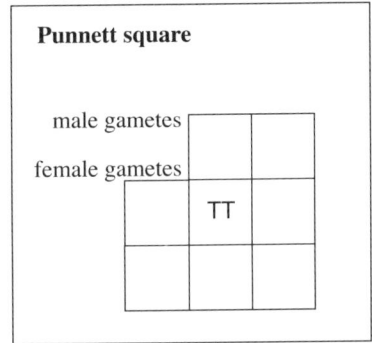

Punnett square		

male gametes

female gametes

	TT	

5 a The table shows one possible system of crop rotation used in agriculture.

Field	Year 1	Year 2	Year 3	Year 4
A	Sprouts	Peas	Potatoes	Fallow or cereal
B	Fallow or cereal	Sprouts	Peas	Potatoes
C	Peas	Potatoes	Fallow or cereal	Sprouts

i Write out the likely sequence of a fourth field, field D *(1)*

ii What is meant by the term 'crop rotation'? *(2)*

b The level of nitrate in the soil can be measured.
The values obtained for the sprout and the pea fields are shown in this table:

Crop	Field	Nitrate level in soil/arbitrary units
peas	A	82
peas	B	88
peas	C	80
sprouts	A	54
sprouts	B	44
sprouts	C	52

i Draw a bar chart of these results *(3)*

ii Calculate the percentage increase in nitrate level when peas are grown. Show your working. *(3)*

c The farmer can protect the crops using insecticides or using a biological control system.

i What is meant by biological control? *(1)*

ii Give two reasons why using biological control would be preferable to using insecticides. *(2)*

6 **a** Draw a simple diagram to explain the meaning of the term global warming. *(3)*
  b Name two different greenhouse gases. *(2)*
  c Explain how global warming might affect:
   i sea level
   ii the pattern of insect pest distribution around the world
   iii the likelihood of gales and storms. *(3 x 2)*

7 This shows a human red blood cell, a cell from the liver and a palisade cell from a leaf.

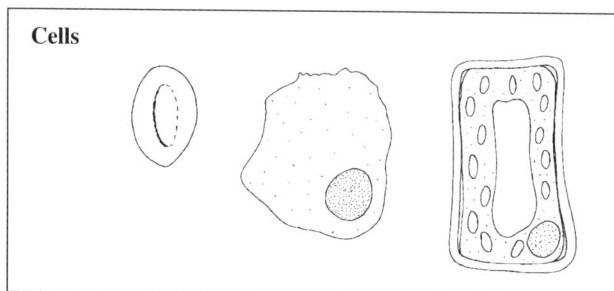

  a Name one structure found in two of the cells but not in the other. *(1)*
  b Name a structure found in one cell that allows it to carry out photosynthesis. *(1)*
  c Name one other cell found in a plant, and state its function. *(2)*
  d Red blood cells are very specialised. What is meant by specialisation? *(1)*
  e How are red blood cells specialised? *(2)*

8 The diagram shows the amount of DNA in a cell during cell division.

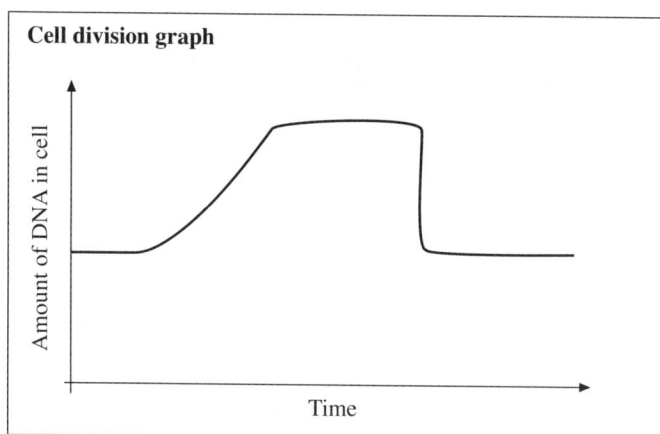

  a Name the type of cell division occurring in the cell.
   Explain how you arrived at your answer. *(2)*
  b What is the function of DNA? *(2)*
  c The DNA content of a cell may be altered as a result of radiation.
   What name is given to this kind of change in a cell's DNA? *(1)*
  d The DNA content of a cell may also be changed deliberately, by genetic engineering.
   Use the following terms to explain this technique. *(5)*

   bacterium, clone, plasmid, restriction enzyme, ligase

1   The diagram shows an experiment to investigate the effect of carbon dioxide
    concentration on the rate of photosynthesis.

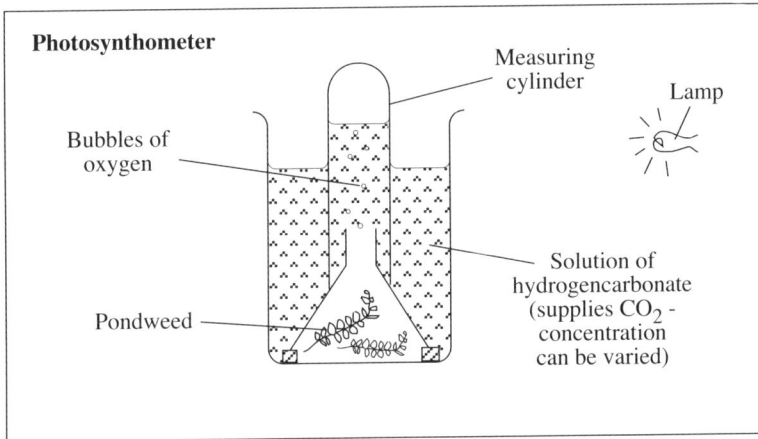

a   Why is it important that the lamp is not moved during the experiment?   *(1)*
b   Suggest a suitable control for this experiment. Explain why this is a good control. *(2)*
c   The experiment was repeated at two different temperatures.
    The results are shown in the graph below:

i   Which factor is limiting the rate of
    photosynthesis at A?   *(1)*
ii Which factor is limiting the rate of
    photosynthesis at B?   *(1)*
d   Greenhouse owners sometimes use
    paraffin-burning stoves in their greenhouses.
    Give two reasons why this is a benefit. *(2)*
e   Many plant growers water their plants
    with a solution containing nitrate.
    Why is nitrate important in plant growth? *(1)*

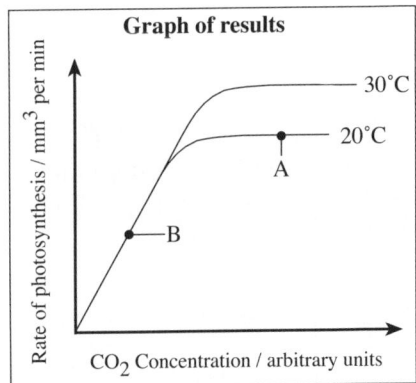

2   The diagram shows the sequence of division in a cell.

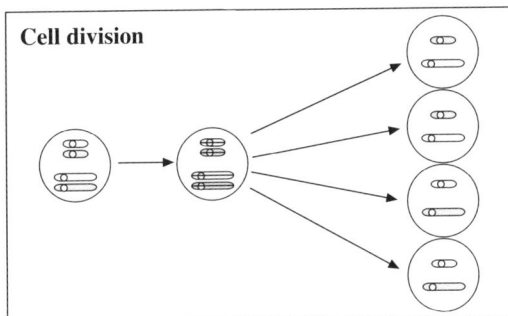

a Name the type of cell division shown in the diagram. *(1)*
b What is the diploid number of chromosomes in these cells? *(1)*
c Explain the importance of this type of cell division in the life of a mammal. *(3)*

The diagram shows a short section of DNA.

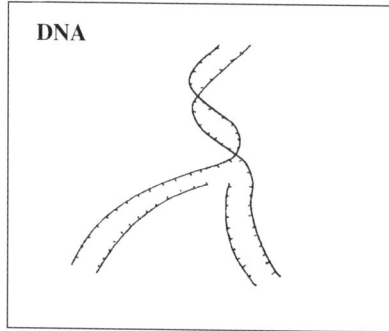

d Name the process shown in the diagram. *(1)*
e Where is DNA found in a cell? *(1)*
f What name is given to a short section of DNA? *(1)*
g Explain how DNA controls the characteristics of
    living organisms. *(4)*

3 The diagram shows some of the stages involved in making beer.

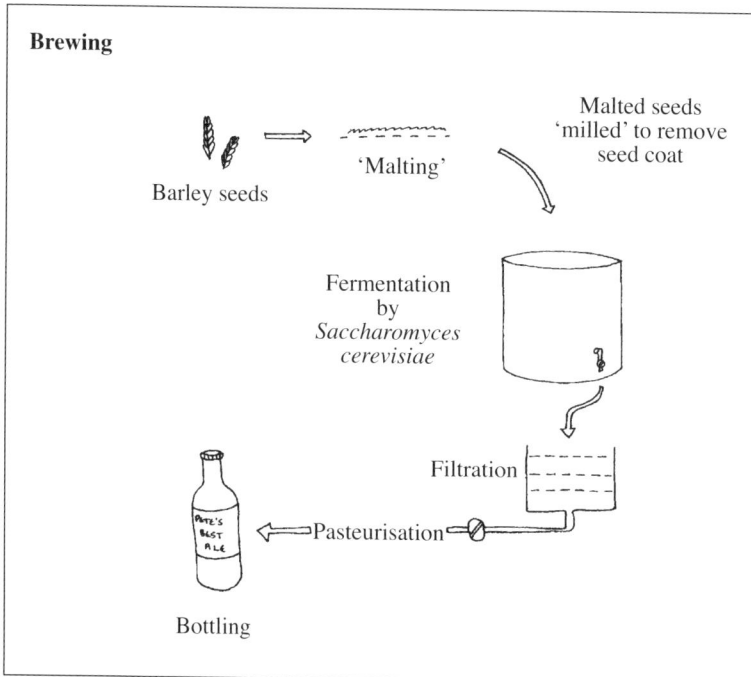

During the malting stage the barley seeds germinate.
Starch in the seeds is converted to maltose.

a Suggest two environmental conditions required for malting. *(2)*
b Name the enzyme responsible for converting starch to maltose. *(1)*
c Name the genus of the organism responsible for the fermentation process. *(1)*

The rate of alcohol production depends on the temperature in the fermentation vat.
The results in the table were collected from an experiment designed to test this effect of temperature.

Temperature / °C	10	20	30	40	50	60
Rate of alcohol production / units of alcohol per hour	0.5	1.4	2.7	3.5	2.3	0.0

d Plot a graph of this information. *(4)*
e Calculate the increase in alcohol production between 25°C and 35°C. *(1)*
f Explain the result of heating the mixture to 60°C. *(2)*
g Suggest why the beer is pasteurised before it is bottled. *(1)*
h Name the gas that gives the 'fizz' to bottled beer. *(1)*

4 The diagram shows a fermenter that may be used to commercially produce an antibiotic.
The culture medium is infected with an aerobic antibiotic-producing mould.

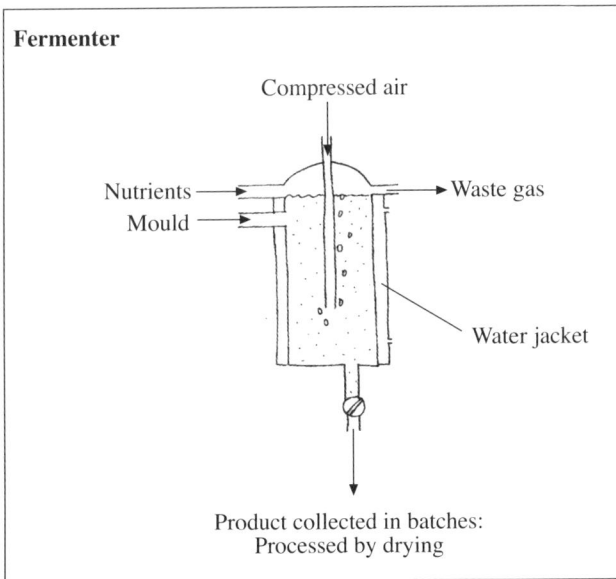

Fermenter

Compressed air

Nutrients →
Mould →

→ Waste gas

Water jacket

Product collected in batches:
Processed by drying

a What is meant by the term 'aerobic'? *(1)*
b Why is it necessary to supply the mould with glucose? *(1)*
c Suggest one reason why the antibiotic is dried and crystallised once the contents of the fermenter have been collected. *(1)*
d Name one antibiotic that could be produced in this system. *(1)*

Sore throats are sometimes caused by a bacterium called *Streptococcus*.
This type of sore throat can be treated with an antibiotic, but there is a danger
that the bacterium can develop a resistance to the antibiotic.
The diagram shows how an antibiotic-resistant form may develop.

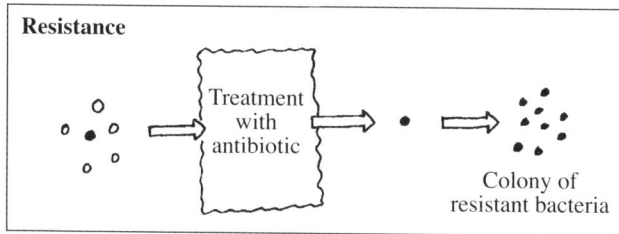

Resistance

Treatment with antibiotic

Colony of resistant bacteria

e   Name the process which leads to the formation of the antibiotic-resistant bacterium. *(1)*
f   Name the process which leads to the development of a colony of antibiotic-resistant
bacteria whilst killing off the non-resistant bacterial cells. *(1)*
g   Explain the difference between an antiseptic and an antibiotic. *(2)*

5   Jack has been told that he has red-green colour blindness.
This condition is caused by a mutation in a single gene, carried on the X chromosome.

a   Suggest one symptom of red-green colour blindness. *(1)*
b   Give one cause of mutations in genes. *(1)*
c   Jack is married to Helen. They have three children – one of them, Anita, is also
red-green colour blind. What is the genotype of Helen with respect to this single gene?
Use a suitable genetic diagram to explain how you arrived at your answer. *(4)*
d   Red-green colour blindness also occurs in some South American monkeys.
These monkeys live high in the rainforest, and feed almost completely on fruits.
Explain why the frequency of the mutated gene is falling in these monkey
populations. *(4)*

6   Global warming has led to changes in weather patterns, including very heavy rainfall.
One result of this has been flooding in some parts of this country.
This flooding may sometimes allow sewage to get into rivers and lakes.
As a result many fish and other aquatic organisms die.

a   Explain how this sewage pollution causes fish to die. *(4)*
b   Water treatment plants (sewage farms) try to remove sewage from water before
it is allowed to enter rivers.
One of the final stages in the treatment process is to add chlorine to the water.
What is the reason for this? *(2)*
c   The dried remains of the sewage treatment may be sold.
What are they used for? *(1)*

1 Seeds will only germinate if the environmental conditions are suitable.
   This experiment was set up to investigate the conditions required for germination

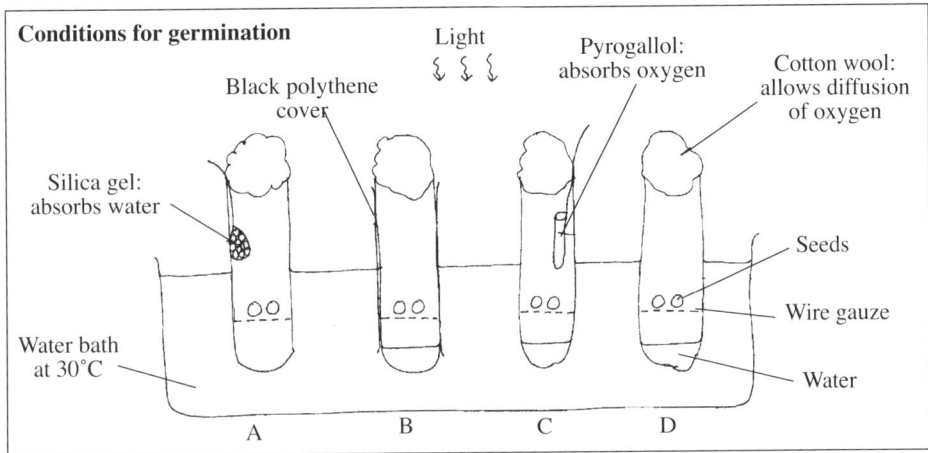

a In which of the tubes, A to D, will the seeds germinate? Explain your answer.   *(4)*
b These results were obtained from an experiment to show that seed germination is
   affected by temperature. Seven lots of 100 seeds were kept on moist cotton wool
   and subjected to different temperatures. After 48 hours the number showing
   germination (at least 1 mm of root showing) were counted.

Temperature/°C	Percentage germination
5	3
15	22
25	55
35	79
45	52
55	19
65	2

c Present the results in a graph   *(3)*
d What does the shape of the graph tell you about the control of germination
   in mustard seeds?   *(2)*
e Why do gardeners sometimes scratch a hole in the seed coat before planting?   *(1)*

2 The diagram on the next page shows a kidney machine that is used to remove waste
   products from the blood plasma.

a Name one dangerous substance present in the blood plasma which would be
   removed by the dialysis machine.   *(1)*
b Name the process by which this substance moves from blood plasma to
   dialysis fluid.   *(1)*
c Explain the importance of preventing air bubbles entering the patient's
   blood system.   *(1)*

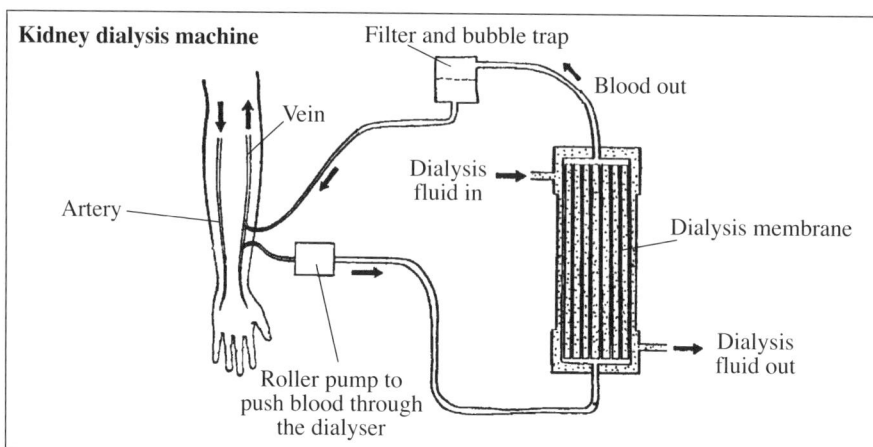

Kidney dialysis machine

Filter and bubble trap

Blood out

Vein

Dialysis fluid in

Artery

Dialysis membrane

Dialysis fluid out

Roller pump to push blood through the dialyser

Doctors prefer to perform a kidney transplant rather than continue dialysis for many years. There is some possibility that a transplanted kidney will be rejected.

d Describe how doctors try to reduce the risks of rejection of a transplanted kidney. *(3)*

e What are the advantages and disadvantages to a patient of having a kidney transplant rather than dialysis treatment? *(4)*

3 Cystic fibrosis is a serious condition in Humans. Many of the body tubes become blocked with a very sticky mucus. Bacteria invade the mucus and cause serious infections, and tubes and passageways blocked by the mucus do not allow the passage of important juices. Organs most affected by the condition are the lungs, pancreas and reproductive organs. The disease is inherited, and involves a single gene with two alleles.

Two parents who showed no symptoms of the condition had two children. The second child had cystic fibrosis although the other child was healthy.

a Is the allele that causes cystic fibrosis dominant or recessive? Explain your answer. *(2)*

b The parents decide to have another child. What is the chance that the third child will have cystic fibrosis? Use a genetic diagram to explain your answer. *(4)*

c The condition is treated by giving patients antibiotics and capsules of enzymes. Explain why this treatment is effective. *(2)*

Read this extract from a scientific journal.

"Medical researchers have developed a method for correcting cystic fibrosis. The treatment involves introducing a normal allele of the gene for a salt-transporting protein into the lungs of patients suffering from this condition. The normal gene is inserted into the coat of a virus similar to the one which causes the common cold. The virus' own genetic material is removed. The patient inhales the genetically-engineered virus, the lung cells are invaded by the virus and stop producing the sticky mucus."

d Draw a series of diagrams to explain how the virus could be genetically engineered to contain the 'normal' gene. *(4)*

e Why are some people resistant to the use of genetically-engineered organisms? *(3)*

4 During pregnancy, the developing foetus is attached to the mother's body through the placenta. The diagram shows the structure of this organ, and its attachment to the foetus.

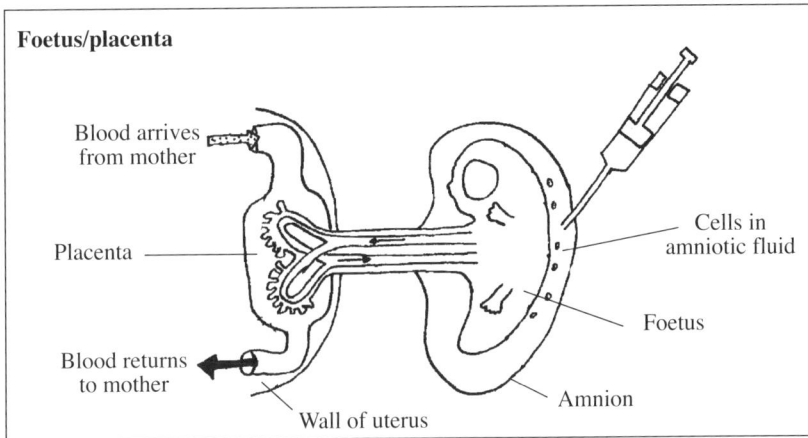

Foetus/placenta
Blood arrives from mother
Placenta
Blood returns to mother
Wall of uterus
Cells in amniotic fluid
Foetus
Amnion

a Name two substances which pass from the foetus to the mother. *(2)*
b How is the structure of the placenta adapted to carry out this transfer? *(2)*
c Name two organs, in the baby's body, which take over the functions of the placenta once the baby is born.
State the functions that these organs will perform. *(2)*

A technique called *amniocentesis* can be used to check the genotype of the foetus.
In this technique, a sample of amniotic fluid is removed using a long needle.
The fluid contains cells shed from the body of the foetus.
The cells can be stained, squashed and their chromosomes examined using a microscope.

d What is the function of amniotic fluid? *(1)*
e Which condition would the baby have if the microscopist counted an extra chromosome 21? *(1)*

Scientists have been able to count the number of these abnormal chromosomes in mothers of different ages. The results are shown in the table:

Age of mother/years	20-24	25-29	30-34	35-39	40-44	45-49
Frequency of abnormal foetus/per 1000 females	0.5	2.8	4.9	9.9	19.8	27.2

f Plot this information as a bar graph. *(3)*
g What is the percentage increase in abnormal foetuses between the age groups 30-34 and 45-49? Show your working. *(2)*
h Women may be given Hormone Replacement Therapy to delay the onset of menopause.
Give one possible benefit and one possible disadvantage of this treatment. *(2)*

5 Posters in a doctor's surgery describe a variety of diseases.
Some diseases described in this way are included in this list.

AIDS, anaemia, athlete's foot, diabetes, measles, coronary heart disease, rickets, tuberculosis

a Use this list to name:

    i a disease caused by a bacterium
    ii a disease caused by a virus
    iii a vitamin-deficiency disease
    iv a disease that can be treated with a fungicide   *(4)*

The body can respond to attack by pathogens (disease-causing organisms).
The flow diagram shows how disease-fighting cells are produced.

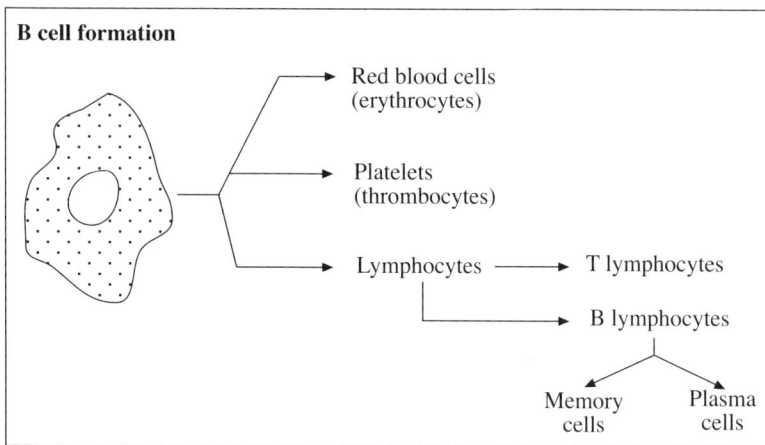

b Explain how B cells protect the body from pathogens.   *(3)*
c The graph shows the antibody concentration in the blood following an injection of a flu vaccine. Copy and complete the graph to show the effect of an infection by the influenza virus at week 6.   *(3)*

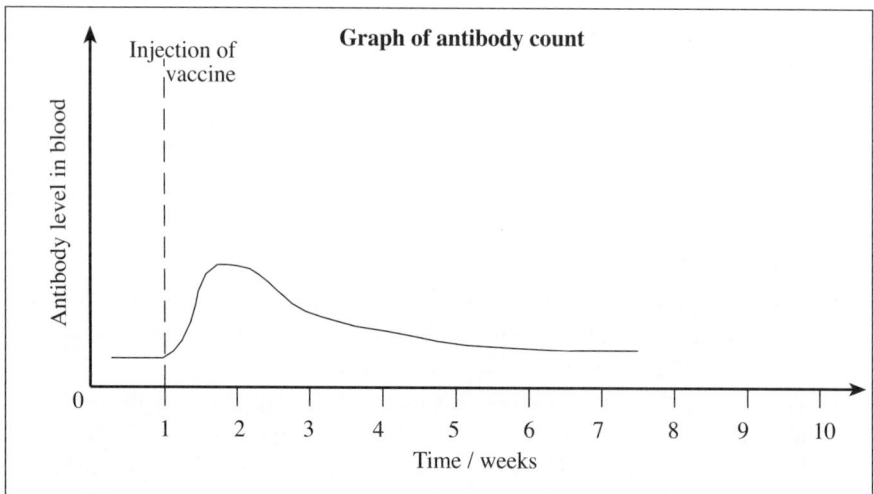